God Ain't Done With Me Yet:
Me Yet:
Uniquely Blessed

By: Sherria Young

DEDICATION

This book is dedicated to my loving and devoted mother Robin, my darling son, Joshua, whom I truly adore , and my family and friends. Thank you for reading the incredible story of the amazing life that God has given me. God Ain't Done with me Yet: Uniquelyblssed will not only inspire you, but you will be educated, encouraged, and immensely blessed.

CONTENTS

ACKNOWLEDGMENTS

Giving honor to my Lord and Savior, Jesus Christ, who is the head of my life. I would like to thank God for allowing me to have an opportunity to share my testimony through the writing in this book and to be a blessing to others. Lord, you gave me the strength and faith as I wrote this book although it is not easy exposing the things that have happened in my life. Thank you, for giving me the courage and boldness to come forth in breaking the silence so that others will read this story and know that you can do anything you put your mind to. If you believe, you can achieve and be blessed.

To my awesome and loving parents, I thank you for the wisdom, love and support you've given me. Mom, I am so grateful to have you as my mom. You mean the world to me and I am so blessed to have you in my life. I thank God for you making me the person I am today. You could have decided to give me away to an orphanage, foster care, adoption, or a family member. Instead you trusted God and raised me to be a beautiful intelligent daughter! For that reason, I accomplished my goals and dreams while making a difference in the lives of others. Mom, you are the best! I love you with all of my heart!

To my handsome and wonderful son: Thank you for entrusting me, as your blind mother and never feeling I was different from other moms. I shall continue to provide you with spiritual growth, love, hope, encouragement, and determination to do your best in achieving your goals and dreams. You are my pride and joy! "Every good and perfect gift is from above."

To my favorite Auntie Marilyn: thank you for always lending an ear when I needed someone to talk to, even as I spoke conversations that were graphic, you laughed, said, "You are my baby, my niece, my brother's child. Where did you come from?" Thank you for being there and supporting me in school, graduation and through life's challenges. Thank you for understanding when no one else could understand. Thank you for assisting me with putting both book titles together. Grandly, appreciated. It is so beautiful! I love you to the moon and back.

To my "other" parents: thank you Sandy and Dawn for all the support you've given whether financially or emotionally, and even caring for the little guy while I was working. I will love you all always and cherish my other mother in my heart forever.

To all of my devoted proofreaders and editors: Thank you for the love and support you've shown me as you, tirelessly, worked to prepare this wonderful book of my life. I am forever grateful for each and every one of you.

Love always,

Uniquelyblessed1

Introduction

Uniquelyblessed1, as I call myself, was born 6 months premature to parents Robin and James. While I was an infant, in the hospital, I had to stay in an incubator to receive oxygen for 3 months because my lungs weren't fully developed. As a result of the physicians administering too much oxygen I was diagnosed with Retinopathy of Prematurity, which caused my blindness.

After hearing the devastating news from doctors, can you imagine how my parents must have felt? Robin and James, my loving parents had all kinds of thoughts going through their minds. They had questions like," how are we going to raise a blind child? Would she be able to attend public school? Do we treat her like we would treat a normal child and give her the same things that we give to a sighted child such as a bike? My parents, I am told, were nervous, fearful, filled with tears, depressed, and full of unanswered questions. The simple answer to their multitude questions was "Yes, treat Uniquelyblessed1 just like you would a normal child, although some things would need to be done, differently.

With much prayer both parents knew that their precious child was a gift from God. According to the word of God in James 1: 17, it is stated, "Every good and perfect gift comes from above." Robin and James knew that their daughter was a blessing from God. They knew she would be talented, have the ability to sing, become a child of God, and be educated.

The author admires her mother and thanks the Lord that Robin, her Mom, decided to raise her daughter. She could have given Uniquelyblessed1 up for an adoption or sent her to foster care. Uniquelyblessed1's mom knew her child was a blessing from God. Although Robin's eyes were filled with tears as she suffered from depression, and was afraid, she knew that all of her help would come from the Lord, which is found in Psalms 121. Robin was happy that God blessed her with a beautiful baby girl who would be wise, sophisticated, and above all God would allow happiness and strength while ensuring all of Uniquelyblessed1's needs were met. God's words tell us in Nehemiah 8: 10 speaks the joy of the Lord is your strength. "Believe it, receive, it, and claim it in Jesus' name."

Uniquelyblessed1 wrote this book concerning her life because she wants her testimony to be a blessing to someone else. You never know what a person is going through. In Philippians 4 verse 13 tells us that I can do all things through Christ who strengthens me. No matter what comes your way, believe in your higher power! Why, because he's the only one who can give you that strength to stand the test and trials in your life. "You never know how your testimony may be a blessing to someone else", she'd say.

1

UNIQUELY BLESSED AS A CHILD

I was born to Robin and James in July 1980. After I was born 6 months early, a pound and 11 ounces, Robin and James were informed that I had to be administered oxygen because my lungs weren't fully developed, due to prematurity. As the result of too much oxygen, I was diagnosed with Retinopathy and prematurity, which ultimately caused my blindness. According to my aunt Jamaica, "I was the size of a cricket; I could fit in the palm of your hand." I was so tiny and my mom said "I could fit in a shoe box." As you read this story, you will say wow! Look at her now because God held uniquelyblessed1 in the palm of his hand. This is why I call myself "The miracle baby."

In 3 months, I was able to go home with my family. My family knew that much prayer and trusting in God would help them get through this difficult situation. At the age of 6 months old, I received physical therapy as well as occupational therapy to gain strength in muscles, gross motor skills, and I learned to recognize different sounds and objects using the light perception and shadows that was left in my right eye.

Robin and James had a baby girl 3 years after Uniquelyblessed1 was conceived. Baby girl was given the name Sarah. Sarah was fully sighted. Both children were treated equally. If Sarah received a bike, uniquelyblessed1 received one, as well. Sarah and Uniquelyblessed1 learned how to ride bikes with training wheels. If Uniquelyblessed1 ran into a pole, she remembered that the pole was there, and knew not to run into it again while riding her bike. One day, my youngest sister and I were fighting in mom's living room. Why did we do that? All of a sudden, we heard " Boom!".… My mother had these pretty glass swans that fell on the floor and broke. She was extremely angry with us. Sarah cared about her visually impaired sister a lot. However, she did not appreciate people staring at me, due to my blindness. " It's ok", I said, " Ignore those people. As long as they don't put their hands on me, that's all that matters." Eventually she calmed down and went on with the day. Sarah says that I'm the responsible one, never looking for help, very independent, and many are inspired by me. Sarah loves me very much.

*(Sarah, my dad James, and I sitting together)

When my sister, Sarah was older, in 2016 she married the love of her life! She had a girl and boy named Keith and Kelly. My niece and nephew adored me, their Auntie and I, in return, love them to pieces. My grandmother, Ruth, played a major role in my life. Although Grandma Ruth loved all of her grandchildren, often, she would speak very highly of me, when communicating with family and coworkers often, while working at Domino sugar. Grandma always talked about my accomplishments and she was over protective. Grandma wanted the best for me and she would say make sure I have everything I needed. She would wonder if "she's alright in the tub… Does she need me to bathe her? Did she eat today? Go get her. .." I would always respond with "Mom tell Grandma I'm alright, I don't need any help. I'm not a baby." I knew my grandma loved and cared about me, but was and very over protected.

Grandma even wanted me to have a seeing eye dog. However, I, simply didn't want a dog because it's like taking care of a child and a big expense, I thought. Grandma felt that having this dog would be protection for me. Grandma Ruth had 2 girls Robin and Elaine, 4 grandchildren; Sarah, Karen, Sheron, and I, 5 great Grandchildren; Joshua, who was my son along with, Keith and Kelly who are Sarah's children, and Tia and Dan, who were Karen's children. She also went to church every Sunday. Afterwards, the family dined with one another as they shared stories, nursery rhymes, sang songs, and watched favorite tv shows. This is a close knitted family that loves God as well as each other, loves family gatherings, food, dancing, and music.

"Around Christmas time, the family enjoyed the aroma of Grandma's delicious chocolate chip cookies and homemade pound cake. Grandma could make some baked Mac and cheese! As you come in the door of Grandma's house, smelling her delicious cooking, you always heard her singing in her opera voice or yelling. " who is that…" as she waits for a response while walking from the kitchen to the front door. Grandma looked forward to having her family and grandchildren over during the holiday especially, Christmas. She loved to decorate the inside and outside of her home, as she placed gifts under tree with moving trains around them. Each grandchild had a stocking stuffer that was hung on the fireplace. We knew we could find some goodies in our stockings! Grandma loved scratching hair and cleaning wax out of your ears. She was something special. Grandma received her crown in glory in April of 2011. I wrote the following poem for the family to my grandma;

SHERRIA YOUNG

AN ANGEL FROM HEAVEN ABOVE

On an early bright Sunday morning
God called an angel whom we love to heaven above
Her spirit will always linger near even when we shed a tear
In our hearts she'll be remembered so dear
We'll remember her beautiful smile
While working in the kitchen with all her cooking styles
Preparing her special dishes like sweet potatoes, collard greens
Mac and cheese as she sung her favorite tunes
We'll remember the good times we shared
From a Grandmother who always cared
Now that she is gone, her hugs and kisses shall continue on
We'll send her up a kiss to let her know that she will be missed
Love your grandchildren/great grandchildren

In my family we believed that "a family that prays together, stays together.

* (A surprise birthday celebration for Grandma Wright)

Growing up as a child was a joy for me. At an early age, I accepted Jesus Christ as Lord and savior under the leadership of the current pastor Marshall. F. Prentice., Zion Baptist Church. I have a passion to sing and a beautiful voice used in ministry. My voice soothes a person's soul as tears flows from one's eyes. My voice is one that will restore and win souls to Christ. I've sung with my youth choir at church and continues to sing on the Youth and Young Adult Choir today. I've directed a youth choir of my best friend Mia grandmother's church called Ministry of Multitudes Apostolic Church. I co-directed the Sounds of Praise Gospel Choir, where blind individuals from various churches/denominations sang to win souls to Christ. Not only have I sang at my church; I also sing with the Reunion Choir of Baltimore while performing solos in weddings, talent shows, funerals, and concerts. I've worked with children in the nursery, courtesy guile, which welcome visitors, attends bible study/Sunday school, praise and worship. Me, a blind woman taught kindergarten at a Christian camp, youth learned songs, bible scriptures, numbers, days of the week, calendar, as well as the alphabet.

I experienced more than the average child who is sighted. As a result of the people who love and cared about me, journeyed around the world to Nassau/Free Port Bahamas, St Johns Canada, Dominican Republic, Cancun Mexico , Denver Colorado, Delaware, Los Angeles California Detroit Michigan, Orlando/Orange Park/Lakeland/Kissimmee Florida Harrisburg/Shrewsbury/Hanover/Redding Pennsylvania, Norfolk/Cull Pepper/Williams Burg Virginia, Atlanta/Buckhead/Suwanee/Buford/Brazelton/Lawrenceville Georgia, Long Island/Staten Island New York, Charlotte/Raleigh/Smithfield/Greensboro/Greenville/Winston Salem

North Carolina, Washington DC, Dallas Tx, East Orange/Plainfield New Jersey, Cincinnati Ohio, Louwville Kentucky, Annapolis, Ocean City, and Solomon Island Maryland.

As you can see, being blind does not stop you from living your dreams. Believe me, you have not experienced a vacation until you have taken a cruise. It was a blast to visit Grand Turk island, Half Moon K, St Johns Canada and the Bahamas one more time. While on the cruise, we were able to view different countries, comedy shows, movies, swimming pool, basketball court, ice sculptures, gym, an arcade, Casino, adult/kid clubs, play bingo, and a variety of dining places to eat. They even had a romantic lounge for couples. Those cruises were amazing! I enjoy traveling and believe me, "there's more to life than Baltimore." If you have eyes to see and ears to hear get out and see the World." **Live life to the fullest because, Life is only what you make it!"**

I remember when I was 4 years old, I held my cousin, James. He was the first child I have ever held. James was named after my dad, which is his sister's child. Her name is Aunt Marilyn. Marilyn is my favorite aunt and we are very close. Aunt Marilyn is supportive and one I can always count on. Marilyn, affectionately calls her niece(me of course)," Ray Ray," and loves me to the moon and back. One day James started crying. I picked him up and rocked him in my arms. The crying ceased. Aunt Marilyn couldn't believe it. She thought to herself, "I know I just heard my baby crying. Where is he?" She then looked at me and realized, her blind niece had the infant cradled in her arms as she sang . To this day we all still talk about that very moment. I asked my aunt to write about what it was like for her to have a blind niece and what it has been like having me as a niece throughout the years.

I was 15 when Uniquelyblessed1 was born. And what I remember most about her birth was the reactions of my brother James and my parents. I come from a family of prayers so there was a lot of praying for healing and predictions that Uniquelyblessed1 would be able to see. Over the course of many years, I wondered what the miracle would be that would give Uniquelyblessed1 sight.

As I write this forward, I feel like I have the answer to that question. Sight for Uniquelyblessed1 is not what she has been able to see with her eyes. It is the insight she has developed throughout her life that has made her determined to the point of appearing to be the stubborn woman she is. Even as a toddler, she did not seem to hear warnings of stop, you can't do that. I think she grew accustomed to trying to beat us to the punch. So to speak before she could be stopped from doing what she had her mind set to do.

One incident that stands out for me, although there were many occurred when I was 4 years old. My son James, named after my brother and I lived with Uniquelyblessed1, her mom Robin, and youngest sister Sarah. One afternoon, Robin was able to sing and rock James to sleep. A miracle within itself because the boy treated sleep like it was something he was allergic too. Robin and I both went to check on Robert James as Uniquelyblessed1 called him and Uniquelyblessed1 was holding and rocking him. Through our shock, We asked how she was able to pick up a baby without help and why she had picked him up. She said he started to cry and I felt around until I found him and I picked him up. We were torn between shock over a 4 year old without sight managing to safely pick up a baby from his bed Holding him correctly and trying to decide if she should be disciplined in some way because we had already told her she could not hold the baby.

I tell this story as a summary of how Uniquelyblessed1 has been from the beginning of life. It has always been as if even as a baby, any hint from anyone that she could not or should not do something became a challenge with Uniquelyblessed1 as the ultimate victor, survivor, walking independently at an early age, motherhood, college, work, travel, you name it. If it was something she wanted to do, she has done it.

One of the proudest days of my life, was when I graduated college with an undergraduate degree. It is the same day Uniquelyblessed1 graduated from the same school at the same time with a graduate degree. Uniquelyblessed1 has been a testament to our family and I hope she will be to you as well. But often, you are told you can't because of the fear and or ignorance as unintentional as it may be of those around you. Not because of your lack of ability. If you want it, don't let someone's else's fear stop you from at least trying. If you fail the first time, put some ice on those bruises and try again.

Uniquelyblessed1, I love you and I admire your strength, tenacity, compassion and intelligence. I pray that your book exceeds your wildest expectations. You have spent so many years helping others. Now, it is time for you! Best of luck, with all my heart, Aunt Marilyn.

James now, has a baby boy who is so handsome and chunky. On James's birthday he received a nice little reminder… "I remember holding you when you were little. "I was the only one who could get you to stop crying." Wow! He's all grown up now! He's an excellent proud father, who, loves his son with all of his heart.

* (Me and Auntie Marilyn)

I, also watched my cousin, Marcy. Marcy (MOODA) was crazy about, me.! From the time she was an infant to the present. When Marcy was around 3 years old, she knew she was going with me for the weekend.

Marcy sat at the front door with her bookbag waiting patiently for me to arrive. Once I got there, she would run up, wrap her legs around me so that I could pick her up to give her a hug. Marcy loved herself some me. We were excited to see one another. Marcy's mother Marcia never looked at me as if I was blind. She used to joke and say "you not blind, you just getting a check. You can see," and we laughed. Marcia is my cousin's daughter's mother but she's still family to me. To me, "Being blind is not a handicapped, it's a condition."

Children are dear to my heart.. Another one of my cousins asked me to babysit often. She had two children, Tina and Luke. Mandy's opinion is, "my experience opened me up to be more open to people with disabilities. I realized that my blind cousin has a passion for children and she's special. People with disabilities have ways of gaining strength, often times more than those without disabilities. Mandy knew I was trustworthy. Otherwise she would not have allowed me to watch her 'damned' kids. My cousin doesn't mind saying what's on her mind. You will definitely get a kick out of it and you will know that she is serious. But she always speaks the truth.

James had another daughter named Meggan who is 3 years older than me. All 3 girls grew up together and loved one another. Meggan and I had fun at birthday parties and, bowling, although communicating with each other via phone or in person is what we favored most. One day Meggan and I were walking down the street and she ran me in to a pole. It wasn't on purpose but she felt so bad. Meggan hugged me so many times, asking are you okay as she rubs my forehead. I replied "yes, girl I'm alright. It was just a mistake." Today we laugh and joke about it. Meggan is the oldest sister from my biological father who at times tries to be my mother telling me what to do and not to do. You can't help but to love her!!! Meggan is married. She and her husband Tom have a son named Kevin. Sarah,

Meggan, and I have children that are within a year of each other.

My Mom, Robin has a passion towards nursing rendering quality patient care to relatives in addition to the elderly from private duty settings, nursing homes, hospice care, or home health care. Robin is dedicated to her family and friends and doesn't mind lending a helping hand to someone in need. My mom is an excellent cook; everyone runs to our house to get a plate. Her food is delicious! Nobody can burn like my mama!!! Robin is a strong individual who has been caring for her family for years. Several of them transitioned to their heavenly home. These included Robin's husband, sister, great grandmother, mother, father, aunts, uncle, cousin, and friends. Watching the transition was very difficult but only the strong survive. Mommy is loving, full of fun, can dance, do anything in the world for anyone, but she isn't one to be reckoned with and she takes no crap from anyone. My dad was a peace maker. He wrestled at Lake Clifton High School. My daddy was good with his hands and a great cook also.

He worked on cars, in home improvement construction, and was a bartender. He delivered televisions for Johnson Brothers, which is now out of business. He was a civilian of the US army and didn't take no stuff off of anyone. He loved and protected his family, specifically his mother. In 1984, God called James home to eternity due to an accident caused by a drunk driver. I cried and would often ask why would someone do such a horrible thing to my daddy? Often, I would say, " I want my daddy. "This was difficult for the family to get through. With much support and prayer, the family healed. God's word speaks of being sad due to death but there will be joy, to God be the glory! Psalms 30.5 tells us that "weeping endure for a night but joy cometh in the morning."

I received my education in the Baltimore City Public School System and did, exceptionally well. School was pretty easy for me, during my elementary years at Garrett Heights Elementary School. All classwork and homework were written in braille.

What is braille? Braille is used by the blind to read and write. Numbers and letters are made from a combination of 6 dots called a braille cell created by Louis Braille in 1821. A braille writer was used to compute math problems along with a talking calculator. A braille writer is similar to a typewriter. It is a machine that allow the blind to write just like the sighted world. Throughout my education, I used JAWS, (jobs access with speech). This is a screen reader for the blind or visually impaired to read the computer screen using a speech synthesizer or braille display. The user will send a command by pressing a combination of keys using the keyboard to instruct synthesizer or display what to say and speak what changes occur onscreen. Key commands instruct the synthesizer to read, spell a word, or read full line of text, find a string of text, or announce location of cursor or focused item. Users can also use the program to spell check or set up a spread sheet using excel.

Mrs. Dee was my braille resource teacher in elementary school. She has watched me blossom from childhood in to adulthood. According to this wonderful instructor as a child I was a quiet child. I would talk when in the computer lab with 2 other students while working on talking typing. Having to deal with the computers, talking, and the blind students talking all at the same time gave Mrs. Dee a headache every other Friday. The Friday's that we weren't in the computer lab, we learned how to cook with Mrs. Dee. When I became more mature I started looking out for the younger kids. One example is the infants and toddlers program held at Garrett Heights Elementary school. The braille resource teacher used me as an example to train the parents as to what their children could grow into. Parents would be worried so I came in at the age of 9 or 10 years old to show parents that I am capable of caring for myself. Mrs. Dee completed a Study on blind transition going into world of work when she was in grad school. I was part of that study. She asked me what I wanted to be when I grew up and "I replied I didn't want to do anything." "I would sit home and collect my check." After hearing this, I replied wow, doesn't sound like something I would have said. Clearly that's not me now as I have held many jobs and other ventures so that's not my character. Then we traveled to California for the Braille Olympics. I discovered there's more to the world. Per Mrs. Dee "up to that time my world was Baltimore city."

From the age of 10 years old until the age of 18, I participated in track and field. This was located at Western Maryland College. Each blind student was paired with a sighted person where the blind individual was able to run the 25-yard dash, 50-yard dash, play T-ball, basketball, run through an obstacle course, standing long jump, running long jump, and the shot put. I, also participated in the Braille Olympics and had the same opportunities at Universal Studio Park located in Los Angeles California.

The first year I attended this event, my Aunt Jamaica accompanied me due to Robin being afraid to fly on an airplane. Robin didn't want her baby to attend the trip alone. Each sighted person would stand behind the blind person, wait for whistle to blow announce on your mark, get set, go! As a student is holding on to person arm or tube connected to robe. Once individual gets to end of event, they are caught in the arms of sighted person. At the end of track and field along with the braille Olympics, the student is given a trophy for participation. Each person also gets a gold silver or bronze medal for competing in first, second, or third place. Track and field at Western Maryland College is a one-day event. However, the braille Olympics is a weekend event where students and chaperones are hosted by volunteer families in their homes in Los Angeles California.

As a pupil in elementary school the blind had an opportunity to partake in an Easter egg hunt. Eggs are hiding in different places. Children were to listen to beeping sound and find the eggs. Kids had a wonderful time and they loved this event every year. Every year the Easter egg hunt was filmed on the news by news reporter Tony Pagnotti, and an article was placed in the newspaper.

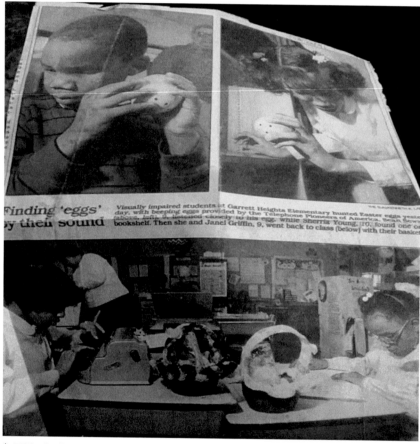

Finding 'eggs' by their sound Visually impaired students at Garrett Heights Elementary hunted Easter eggs yesterday, with beeping eggs provided by the Telephone Pioneers of America. Sean Sewell (above, left), 9, listened closely to his egg, while Sherria Young, 10, found one on a bookshelf. Then she and Janel Griffin, 9, went back to class (below) with their basket

* (Kids finding Easter Eggs during Easter Egg hunt along with article)

After leaving elementary school and entering middle school, I began organizing fund raisers that included bake sales and 50 -50 raffles in order to raise money to attend the trip because it was too expensive for the staff to pay for us. This was when the student realized if she needed or wanted money, sitting home wasn't going to do it. I still travel to this day via train, bus, or plane. The professor wanted to see me incorporate more into the fully sighted world. She wanted me to be more involved outside the blind world. Mrs. Dee felt that I was active within my own community and culture but never formed that special friendship with someone who wasn't blind. According to the professor, I became part of a click in elementary school and it remained for a long time, even in to middle school.

Mrs. Dee asked if I remember one of my instructor's being concerned about me. I replied, I do not; so she began discussing the conversation with me. After listening for a moment, I began to remember. My orientation and mobility teacher was concerned about me being able to maneuver around due to safety reasons and the fact that I was afraid due to blindness. When I was on a stairwell, I would have panic attacks. I don't know if it was because of the big open space or just the sound. Mrs. Dee told her once I get to a certain age I would be motivated and all that would be minute. Sure enough Mrs. Dee was correct. I faced these barriers because my mother was afraid of letting her blind child walk alone outside, or cross the street. She didn't want her child to learn how to catch the bus due to safety reason. This is to be expected from a parent who doesn't know that her child is capable of caring for herself, and she is able to do almost anything a sighted child can do. Robin didn't understand all of this until she received training from several individuals Mrs. Dee, the orientation and mobility instructor, and the National Federation of the Blind.

One year a grant was written by Mrs. Dee for a group of blind students to have a bowling league at the Parkville Bowling Alley, which is now a dental office. The students used bumpers to bowl and enjoyed the league for a year. After bowling, the instructor took the class to Valentino's to have pizza. We loved pizza so that was the best thing ever.

While in school, I was faced with a challenge that I knew I could overcome. I fell behind in all classes, especially in Southeast Middle and Mervo (Mergethaler Vocational-Technical) High school. The work was not in an accessible format. This meant that the work wasn't in braille, textbooks weren't made available in a PDF file, tape, or CD. Therefore, I suffered from exhaustion due to staying up numerous nights completing work. During the last year of high school, I became frustrated and wanted to quit school due to falling behind. I was determined to graduate with my diploma and contacted the board of education, explained story, and a meeting was held at Mervo High School.

Another challenge that I had to deal with was being spit on and hit in the breast while walking from class. Students said things like watch out for that tree while laughing along with jumping over my cane. You are probably thinking," Wow, that poor blind child. She is probably afraid to walk to class or maybe she doesn't want to attend school anymore" I had a strong prayer life and I knew who I belonged to. I was not afraid to walk the halls by myself and I looked forward to attending school, daily.

The word of God says in Isaiah 54:17, "No weapon formed against me shall prosper. King James Version (KJV)" For a long time, I was escorted to every class daily. My friends fought the individual who committed the horrible acts even when asked not to do so. They were so upset with the individuals and couldn't believe they would want to hurt someone like me. Not to brag, but I was the sweetest person you could ever meet. I was described, by my teachers as" humbled and intelligent. I enjoyed helping others, and let nothing stop me from achieving my goals. Robin wanted me to attend the Maryland School for the Blind so she sought help from the National Federation of the blind.

The National Federation of the Blind helps individuals adjust to vision loss and promote participation and integration within the community. Experiences are shared amongst each other to change laws on the state and national level. NFB believes in advocating for independence, education, promoting and protecting the rights of blind people. In order to transform dreams into reality, members work together to have a brighter tomorrow by raising expectations so the blind can have the life they want.

The NFB explained that MSB was a school for blind children with severe handicaps. I received a better education in public school versus a sheltered setting. I asked my mom if I could stay in public school because I wanted to be around my sighted peers, receive a high school diploma, and didn't want to be in a sheltered setting being secluded from the real world. Robin agreed to allow me, her little warrior, to receive my education in the public-school system. "I am so glad my mother allowed me to achieve my goals and dreams. I received my diploma from Baltimore City Public Schools and with the support of my mother, family and friends I am the person that I am today.

Failure was not an option for me. According to Matthew 19:26, "With men things are impossible but with God, all things are possible." I knew that If I continued to trust God and never doubt, he would make it possible for me to graduate with my high school diploma. I kept being determined to succeed while holding on to my faith! Hebrews 11: 1 says," Faith is the substance hope for and the evidence of things not seen." While waiting with the expectation that I was going to complete 12th grade, walk across the stage, and receive my diploma in my hand and make my family and myself proud. I spoke it into the atmosphere, claimed it, believed it, and received it, in Jesus name. I prayed, let go, as I watched God move on my behalf.

A passionate aunt took the responsible role of raising my niece and nephews at the age of 17 years old. This was with the assistance of my parents until my sister Jill was able to care for her children. Jill had 4 children, 2 boys Ethan, Nathan and 2 girls Zoey and April. Family is so important. The children were provided with love and security. Zoey is the youngest and she clung to me. After arriving home from school or work, Zoey ran to me, wrapped herself around my legs so that I would pick her up to give a hug and kiss. She followed her auntie everywhere I went including her medical appointments as well as worship services. Zoey became my shadow. Not only is she my shadow, but also one of my god children. I believe that a strong family builds a foundation, which grows from love, security, and communication. They're so many children who need a loving home when adversity occurs. Would you take your family member into your home like my family and I or would you send them to foster care? It is important that we nurture our children, give them tender love, and care as we watch them mature. Family is so important. Family is everything and I love each and every one of them with all of my heart.

After graduating from high school, I went on to further my education. In December 2002, I received a certificate in Hospitality Culinary Arts and Tourism from Arundel Community College. Not only did I excel in Essex Community College and received an Associates Degree in General studies in May 2003, but also received a Bachelor's Degree in Human Services with a concentration in social work from Sojourner Douglas College with honors in June of 2007. I then decided to continue my education obtaining a master's degree in human services with a concentration in rehabilitation from the University of Baltimore in December of 2011.

* (Me and my aunt Marilyn graduating from college)

"In order to achieve your goals and dreams, you must trust in your higher power and believe you can achieve anything you put your mind too." According to Proverbs 3, verses 5-6 "Trust in the Lord with all thine heart and lean not unto thy own understanding. In all thy ways, acknowledge him, and he shall direct thy paths

Upon completion of my graduate program in human services from University of Baltimore College, I held an internship at a transitional housing program in Baltimore Maryland. This is a transitional housing program for homeless families founded in 2000 that has the capacity to serve 15 families at a time. The program is designed to help families transition from emergency shelters to permanent housing and self-sufficiency. To assist participants in reaching their goals, families are offered intensive case management and participate in support groups, life skills development activities, and parenting classes. They have access to the Career Center to receive employment counseling, job skill training, food pantry, after school and summer programs for children and teens. They are also open to many other networking agencies.

The agency provides a two year stay while providing case management services. Transitional Housing does not give assistance to families with security deposits or eviction funds. However, callers who contact Transitional Housing are given referrals and resources to other agencies such as the Department of Social Services, Mercy Supportive Housing, and First Call for Help, Samaritan Center for BGE Assistance or Eviction assistance or placement. This program provides 8 apartment units that are completely furnished for a family with one or two children. There are seven houses that are fully furnished for a family that has 3 to 5 children. The houses and apartments come with standard appliances such as refrigerator and stove, and central air is in all of the units. No more than 5 children are allowed in the houses.

There is a six month follow up that is done on each client by the Transitional Housing Program. Upon exit of the program the clients can be assisted with services from Mercy Supportive Housing, and the Salvation Army with furniture needs and monetary assistance. Before clients enter the program, they are placed on the Maryland Energy Assistance program better known as M.E.A.P.

Upon leasing a unit in the program, they become a part of a 3-point level system. Level 1 is entry level. Clients adjust with payment of BGE billing and rent, securing appropriate child care, attendance of any support groups if needed. These include substance abuse or mental health. They began community service hours with the program and enter in to employment if not already employed or a training program. Level 2 is compliance with CAC meetings and program requirements, monthly fees paid on time with budget review, monthly case review, and weekly meetings with case manager. Client is to be actively working on their goals, which will engage clients in building life skills. By the end of level 2, all clients must have paid their security deposit. Level 3 is to demonstrate appropriate parenting skills. Clients must maintain compliance with Transitional Housing program rules and regulations. They must be consistent with program fees, family health appointments must be updated, maintained part time or full time employment, and clients should be meeting with case manager for permanent housing options. Director will contact Section 8 for referral of clients, notice of income increased, and permanent housing placement.

Special privileges are given to compliant residents. Monetary assistance in all 3 levels to help the client move forward. Some monies are distributed on a bartering system with the client. The maximum of $20 per client can be borrowed and the client must pay it back within 3 weeks. If not repaid, privileges will be lost. Gift cards and basket of cheers are distributed for compliance and achievements of theirs goals.

Transitional Housing maximizes volunteer involvement, while recognizing personal and spiritual growth which occurs when individuals become personally involved in assisting others. Transitional Housing DePaul serves all people as it sees God's living presence in each individual.

One day I received a called from a perspective client concerning the eligibility requirement of Transitional Housing. The caller was informed that you must be a married family with children or a single parent with children. I also explained to the client that you had to be referred by an agency like Social Services, a shelter or a substance abuse treatment center. The client was made aware of the documents needed for the screening interview. Documents that must be submitted are birth certificate for parent and child, social security card for parent/child, immunization records, and a photo I.D.

After explaining the eligibility process, client began discussing her situation concerning homelessness. Client was evicted as a result of becoming disabled. A physician informed the client to apply for disability benefits. Thereafter, client had to terminate from employment. Although it was difficult for the client to make a decision to apply for benefits, the client knew this was something that had to be done. Client applied for disability benefits.

Client has a minor child and wanted to be in a better situation for her and her child. The client felt that she had no hope and wouldn't amount to anything. She didn't want to accept disability benefits because she wanted to continue to work.

Finally, I explained to the client that she could work as long as physician agreed she was able to work. Client was advised not to think about what she lost but ask yourself what you are going to do to get back on your feet. I also explained that she had to get rid of her pride and ask for help, even though sometimes family members are reluctant to assist with a place to stay. All family members are not like that and you only need a place temporarily until you are accepted into Transitional Housing. Client was inspired and relieved

After giving advice to client, client began to feel like she had confidence within herself. After sharing my story of being disabled and she thanked me for being an inspiration to her. I told client to think positive and be encouraged. We look forward to seeing you at your appointment. Opinion of Uniquelyblessed1, (02/28/2011)

During my internship experience, I had the opportunity to partake in interviewing six perspective clients that came in to Transitional Housing to have their intake eligibility screening done. All clients were interviewed, appropriate documents were submitted with applications, and the requirements as well as the mission of Transitional Housing were explained to the perspective clients. I assisted the Director in the leasing of those clients into their new housing units. Administrative assistance was done with the required Rent Roll that is due on a monthly basis. Financials were reviewed with me through the Director. These included the expenses of managing the maintenance, resident assistance, postage, supplies, transportation, house meetings, telephone, service vendors, mileage reimbursement, and volunteer supplies. The intern also assisted with recording of donors that contributed to the Transitional Housing program.

I was able to meet with clients and they began discussing their problems with me. One client told me that her son was diagnosed with type I diabetes. While at the shelter, I had the opportunity to write a report which consisted of what happen during the 4p.m. to 10 p.m. shift. The report reflected things like one of the staff members brought a cake and ice cream for one of the children's birthday party. Clients and staff sang happy birthday to the child and each staff member as well as the families and their children received cake and ice cream.

Once I had the opportunity to participate with the staff. I felt that the staff member was over stepping her boundaries and that was not her role to question the client. She's not a psychiatrist, therapist or a counselor. Immediately the client became uncomfortable with the level of openness and became hesitant in answering questions that was asked by the staff member of the shelter. The staff should not have questioned the client in that fashion and not only that, the staff member is not even licensed. You don't approach clients in that manner. Then the staff member lied to the client and told her that if she didn't seek mental health assistance because of her mental illness, client's SSI would be denied. Client received psychiatric help and medication as promised. Client has left shelter and moved in to permanent housing.

The staff at shelter and the interns wish client success. I became overwhelmed and the only thing I could say was I'm going home to pray because the whole meeting was unprofessional. I believe this could have been handled in a professional manner. If you refer back to the code of ethics, a person is not to take on a counselor's role if you are not licensed due to breach of confidentiality.

During the meeting staff members along with two interns discussed client issues, change in policy, and rule enforcement. We also discussed the client's need for medication as a result of a mental illness along with disturbing other guests in the shelter. Resolution is that if client doesn't obtain medication within the next week, they will have to leave the program. Child kicked one of the staff members. Client's child needs behavioral health and the parent needs to learn how to control her child. Director of Shelter, (10/04/2011)

Thereafter, the client was brought in to the conference room where client was bombarded with several questions from a staff member of the shelter. The questions consisted of what is depression? Do you know why your depressed? Why is your SSI case pending? I felt that this was unethical I was given the duty to rewrite the policy manual with the assistance of the manager of the shelter.

During my internship I was able to shadow one of the staff members in establishing a transitional plan for one of the clients. Client's plan included goals that were measurable and obtainable. The goals included, finding employment, obtaining and paying for GED, and permanent housing.

The Client has an infant whose been moving from shelter to shelter, residing with family and friends and is looking forward to moving to permanent housing. Client's reason for homelessness is that housing is not affordable without an income. Client wants to get a place of her own. However due to lack of income, I explained to client that they may have to accept transitional housing as an option. I explained to the client that there would be rules that client have to follow and you will receive case management services. Opinion of Uniquelyblessed1, (10/12/2011)

Client agreed to accept transitional housing as the last resort. I referred the client to Transitional Housing and client submitted necessary documentation. I provided client with phone numbers of primary physicians as well as OBGYN's concerning various health issues that needed to be addressed. Client made an appointment to address all medical needs. Client wants to move out of the shelter and into a stable place so she won't have to keep taking her infant outside due to illnesses such as airborne illness, common colds, pneumonia, etc. Client thanked me for all that I have done and recommended that I become a housing counselor for the homeless population. Client is excited and looks forward to moving in to Transitional Housing within one month.

There's a client who has been at the shelter for a week and client has received a job as a nanny. This is an opportunity for client to receive an income but also have a permanent housing for client and child. I am so proud of this client. Client is dedicated and willing to do whatever needs to be done in order to be successful in life. The staff at the shelter as well as myself wish this particular client well.

Overall, I gain a lot of knowledge from the shelter. This was a humbling experience and I want to use the knowledge that I learned in the field of Human Services as well as the internships to bridge the gap with my business. Being able to experience all walks of life concerning homelessness has helped me understand no matter what situation you face in life, never give up, hold on to your faith, and press towards the mark of the high calling of God. Philippians 3:14

* (Bob, my step Father and I)

* (my Parents and all their children)

Robin and Bob became one in June of 1993. Not only does she have two beautiful daughters, now she has 3 step daughters and 2 steps sons. Mark 10: 8 says "... and the two will become one flesh" so they're no longer two, but one flesh." Me, Sarah, Jill, Kim, Pam, Bob Bob Jr, Jim and my mom enjoyed family time, fishing, going to the beach, watching movies, and dining. Jill always made a joke in reference to me being blind. She would say: I believe you can see and you are fooling us. Even though you can't see, you don't let it hinder you from living your life. Some people in the world, if they have a disability, they give up on life. But Jill never seen me sad due to my disability nor did it hinder me. She always seen me travel the world, go to work, and let nothing stop me. Jill says it amazes her that I can do so many things and go so many places. I never let not having sight stop me from doing anything I want to do.

When thinking about people in general that can see and move around and don't have no motivation or drive for themselves. I, on the other hand, have a disability and don't let it hinder me at all. I love that about you Jill Says. "You're very inspirational I love you and I'm glad we became a part of each other's lives." People with disabilities have no fear and they don't let anything stop them. On numerous occasions, Jill stayed up with me persistently assisting with proofreading and making sure formatting of research papers were correct. Even though Jill didn't complete high school or have a college degree, she made sure her blind sister was successful in pursuing a bachelor's degree. From my motivation as well as inspiration, Jill received her high school diploma in may of 2008 and received her degree in Culinary Arts in 2014.

Some individuals don't have integrity and I wonder how they go through life without having any integrity. I have a disability. I don't need people to baby sit me; sometimes I need assistance getting in and out of an automobile and make sure I'm going in the right direction. I recall when a mobility (paratransit) driver came to pick me up and didn't come to assist me to the vehicle, which is part of his/her job duties. What is mobility paratransit? It is a transportation service for the disabled. My brother Bob Jr. realized the mobility driver was negligent and approached him and asked him why he wasn't doing his job the correct way? They got in to an altercation and I intervened to calm him down. The driver apologized and agreed that he should have assisted me to the vehicle. Bob Jr. loves all of his siblings but don't play when it come to his sister who is blind. Remember according to Luke 6:31: states to "treat others as you would want them to treat you."

Bob and Robin were a devoted loving family. Bob, affectionately called Pop-Pop, had a passion for home improvement/construction, and fixing up houses. This was the baddest man in town whether it was texturing ceilings or designing a new home. Everybody loved his creative work. He played ball with his grandsons and watched movies and danced with his granddaughters. Bob spoiled the grandchildren and gave them whatever they wanted. He was a family man who loved God while enjoying worship services prayed every night as he read scriptures from the Bible. Both were married for 23 years until Bob received his crown in glory in 2015. This couple will always be one that is special, loving, and best friends until the end. It hurt so bad when I found out there was nothing else the doctors could do for my Dad. As he was transitioning, I could remember rubbing his arm telling him, "It's ok. You're tired, you can go home now. We will be alright." I began singing it is well with your soul and I told my dad I loved him. I walked out of the room and sat in the waiting room. Once he transitioned, I began having anxiety attacks. I wasn't unaware until one of my family members bought it to my attention.

At this point my emotions were all over the place. I was out of it, although my father prepared me for this. I didn't expect it to be so soon. I thought over and over again: who would have ever thought this would have been the last time to hear your voice? Who would have ever thought this would be the last time to hear you say, " I love you? " I immediately contacted my doctor and I had to take medication temporarily. Bob and I were really close. When you saw one you saw two. We stuck together like glue. Bob was proud of all of his children. He spoke very highly of me due to my accomplishing so much in my life. "Uniquelyblessed1" has done more than people who can see, says Robin and Bob." Both always made sure I was successful in achieving my goals and dreams.

Family is something during and after your loved one has transitioned to the other side. My father was in the hospital on his death bed. His brother's wife worried more about whose name was on the insurance policies? Where are the insurance policies? The children tried to fight me in the hospital on the critical care unit. They told me I disrespected their mother because I replied "that's irrelevant." He's not dead yet, it doesn't matter where they are. I informed the fighters that they could try it if they want too, they would not leave that hospital the same way they came and I gave them a piece of my mind. My mother, then was asked to go outside of the hospital so that they could fight her. This was absolutely ridiculous! This was not the time for all of this to be going on. My father should have been able to go home to glory peacefully. Money is the root to all evil. My father knew who he wanted to leave everything too. He knew that his wife would put him away nicely his son, Bob, and I would take care of whatever else that needed to be done. His family even came to our house and threatened to blow it up. "They did any and everything they could to try to hurt us but didn't succeed." Don't hate me for telling the truth just allow this experience to bless your hearts." Why? Exodus 14: 14 "the Lord Shall fight your battles for you. Ye shall hold your peace." God wants us to know that he fights our battles and will give us peace. When things that are bad happen in our lives, do not be discouraged. The situation that we were challenged with became overwhelming. But I know that my God is Sovereign! He will take care of us. I knew without a shadow of a doubt, He would work it out. In Hebrews 1: 13 God tells us to keep our enemies as our foot stool.

As Christians, we must pray for them love them even when they wrong us. That is easier said than done. You are crazy, after all they have put your family through. Yes indeed, they'll need you before you need them. Things will happen just to see how you are going to react. In our case, we paid for my uncle's funeral arrangements, my Mom assisted my father's baby sister with caring for her husband as he was preparing to go home to glory, my Mom and I helped with preparing the order of service for the funeral as well. I wrote a poem for my aunt. Family come by the house on dad's death anniversary or his birthday to discuss memories as they shed their tears. In spite of what we went through, we forgave them. In Ephesians 4: 32, God says:, "and be kind one to another, tender hearted forgiving one another. Even as God for Christ sake have forgiven you." We did just what Jesus would do.

2

ADULT LIFE BLESSINGS

A Christmas wrapping party was thrown in 2002 by one of my friends Carolyn. Carolyn is Paul's sister and she has a daughter named Carol. She introduced me to her brother Paul and it was all she wrote. He was a handsome man. Paul has the gift of gab and could smooth a woman over. Well, I melted in his arms and we dated for a year.

I discovered I was pregnant in 2003. Paul's true colors began to show. You heard things like," I'm not ready for any more kids. I'm not financially stable. What are you going to do? Are you going to keep it?" My reply, "You should have thought about that before sticking your penis in my vagina or you should have strapped up." Prior to my pregnancy, we discussed if I got pregnant, I would keep it. I don't believe in abortions. He always assured me that if I was to get pregnant, there's nothing to worry about because he would take care of the child. I was sadly mistaken.

At this point Paul exhibited behaviors as a deceiver, liar, cheater, and heartbreaker. While residing in an apartment together the gas and electric was disrupted. Paul received a phone call from a woman stating that she was going on a trip and she needed him to come over to feed her cat. Now we all know what cat needed to be fed... In the meantime his blind girlfriend, me, who was 7 months pregnant was left alone with no lights or electricity and no food. My mother bought me some food, not to mention this was Thanksgiving day. Eventually the lights and electricity were turned back on. I should have learned my lesson from that incident to leave him alone and sadly I did not.

About 3 weeks later, my friend Trina went to get her hair done and I decided to accompany her. As Trina was talking to the hair dresser we realized that she knew Paul. Trina started to explained that we also knew Paul and I was pregnant by him. The hair dresser was in shock because that was supposed to be her boyfriend at the time and she had no knowledge of me. Again, I should have left well enough alone. But what can I say I'm a glutton for punishment. I instantly forgave him and we relocated to another apartment. I had to go out of town on vacation without Paul and asked him to behave while I was gone. I also made a call to Trina to drop in on him to make sure everything was on the up and up. When Trina contacted him and stated that she wanted to purchase some marijuana because they use to smoke together all the time. He told her to come on over. He had her covered. When she got there, she got the shock of her life! There was a stripper in the kitchen cooking in my house like she owned it. Her kids were there as well. Trina played it off while he begged her not to say anything to me. But, of course, as soon as Trina left, she contacted me. I was very hurt but still had the dream of being a family when my son was born. So again I forgave him.

Shortly after that incident my son Joshua was born. It seemed like we were getting back on track. He was treating me better. But that did not last long. He began staying out more and more, telling me he was at a friend's house and not spending anytime with our son. He started making excuses to stay out telling me I was not a good mother, and other hurtful things. I later found out that he had another relationship with a girl who worked up the street at the dollar store. Once I found out who it was, I gave the girl a call to have an adult conversation. She was very disrespectful and seemed to not hear what I had to say. At this point, I was fed up. I told Paul to get out and I did not look back.

* (Joshua and I)

In 2004 I gave birth to a son and name him Joshua All children are gifts from God. When he began to crawl and walk as an infant and I was busy cleaning or cooking, I would place him in the play pen near the area where he could see me until I completed the task. Joshua is a bright intelligent young man. He is a grade ahead and his school recommended that he be skipped when he was in Pre-k. Joshua would read stories to the other class mates because he completed his work so quickly. He received numerous certificates concerning his academics/spelling B's while in catholic school. My aunt who was 18 years old needed assistance with the SAT practice test and Joshua was able to give the assistance that was needed.

I love Joshua with all of my heart and, he is my pride a joy, and thank God for the precious gift he has blessed me with. It gives me great joy to travel around the world with my son, and he loves and looks forward to traveling 3 to 4 times a year. Since infancy, he has traveled with me to places such as Denver Colorado, Ohio, Atlanta Georgia, Washington DC, Kissimmee Orlando and Orange Park Florida, Cull Pepper Virginia, Ocean City, Charlotte/Raleigh/Smithfield North Carolina, Harlem New York, Staten Island New York, Long Island New York, Syracuse New York, Atlantic City, East, Orange, and Plainfield New Jersey, Dominican Republic, resorts Massanutten and Shenandoah Valley, and two cruises.

God has given me the necessary tools and guidance when raising a male. As a blind single parent, I had many challenges that I overcame. I had to administer asthma medication to Joshua when asthma attacks arose. Homework had to be done on a daily basis after school, clothes had to ironed and matched together. You may be asking how does a blind person do all those things? I'm glad you asked. Physicians showed me how to administer the medication using the spacer or syringe. He placed my hand on the nozzle of the inhaler and informed me that it has to be pressed twice after its inserted in the spacer. The spacer is placed over child's nose and mouth so that when the medication is dispensed, it will get into the lungs. Liquid medication is measured into the syringe. Blind individual measures amount needed based on whether it feels heavy or light. If the weight feels heavy, you know it's too much and some has to be poured out. Homework had to be sent through email so that I could assist my child with it. Family, friends, even teachers helped me complete Joshua's homework.

Our clothes were match together using the color identifier. This is a device that identifies colors of an object when it's against the item. The blind will hear a voice saying blue or dark green. You can also use color mates, which are safety pens with shapes to help identify the color. A star on the pen represents blue so you place the pen with the star on the outfit and hang on a hanger. Blind people iron all the time. When ironing, lay clothing flat on ironing board. Then as you're ironing the clothes you take your hand and feel to make sure wrinkles are out. If clothing feels smooth, wrinkles are out. If you can still feel wrinkle or lines in the clothing, iron it over again. My duties to clean my residence are the same as a sighted parent. I had to scrub floors and mop, sweep Hardwood floors, polish furniture, do laundry, and clean windows. I also had to cook meals every night.

In my house, there were Braille markings on the cooking knobs to indicate temperature along with a talking timer to time how long food should be cooked. Braille is also on the microwave. You may ask how does a blind person know when food is done? A blind person is able to tell when food is done once they prod the dish with a fork to make sure it's done.

Grocery shopping was a simpler task. I carried Joshua in his car seat, took transportation and when we arrived at the supermarket, an assistant helped me purchase all items needed. I was blessed with a great support system. My parents, grandparents, Joshua's grandparents Sandy and Dawn, my siblings and Joshua's aunt Carolyn. Joshua's God parents Tracy and Clarence were a great support too. "God always makes a way out of no way." According to Ephesians 6: 4 "Do not provoke your children to anger. But bring them up in the discipline and instruction of the Lord."

In life, no matter what situations you are faced with, such as being a blind single parent like myself and having to deal with your child being abandoned by their father, the child feeling anger and resentment because of the absent parent being uninvolved, uninterested in the child's life, when you know that you have done all you can to encourage the child to stay in contact with the father besides the fact his dad is inconsistent, keep praying, provide correction, with God's instructions and believe God will see you through! "If God can do it for me, I know he can do it for you." And I can truly say, "Lord, I am so grateful for all that you have done for me."

My child grew up in the church, becoming an usher, attends Sunday school, Bible study, and worked on the security ministry. The young man accepted Christ to be his Lord and savior at an early age. What a blessing it is to make Jesus your choice getting baptized at the age of 5 years old; one day before your birthday!!! His Grandma Robin, grandparents Sandy and Dawn, Grandma Ruth, Aunt Jamaica, my grandmother's brother and wife who is uncle Tony and aunt Keisha were all present. Joshua's God parents, Tracy and Clarence, were there, too. Joshua was presented with a Bible and cards and everyone was very majestic.

When Joshua was in the womb I read books, scriptures, sang songs, counted numbers, and said ABC's. After he was born and as he matured every day, I taught him magnetic letters and numbers that were raised after touching them. I read stories using printed Braille books, which had print along with images and their descriptions. I would be able to say there's an image of a dog outside on the porch. Joshua realized I was blind and different from other parents when was around 2 or 3 years old. I remember when Joshua was about 2 years old, he told me to come on in his baby's voice after I asked him to take me to the rental office to pay the rent. There's another time Joshua bent to his knees, took my white cane and lifted it up to hit the curb so that I could step up.

A funny story occurred when Joshua was little. Sitting at his grandmother's house in the kitchen. His grandmother watched him as he was looking at me, handing me a picture that he drew. Grandma Sandy said if you can see the way he's looking at you. He looked at me as if to say, "What the devil is wrong with her? Why is she not taking my picture?" We both started laughing. I took the picture and told him it was beautiful Grandma Sandy loved herself some Joshua and spoiled him rotten as we loved taking photos of her grandchild capturing many memories. His grandparents attended/transported him to and from school, graduations, football games baseball games, and school fashion shows.

Around 8 years of age, Joshua asked me where did babies come from? My response was babies come from the computer. You draw the picture as to how you want the child to look and then you print it. The baby comes out and that's all there is to it. He and I shared the story with grandmother Sandy and we all laughed. Grandma Sandy asked why did you tell that baby that? I replied he's too young to know that right now. That was the best way to explain it. Today if I say I birthed you. Joshua will respond "Nope, I came from a computer;" and we laugh about it each time.

I was the other daughter they didn't have. Sandy and I communicated via phone at least 5-10 times a day laughing, joking and discussing her "Poo." She always knew when I was down and gave an encouraging word to lift me up even after the relationship ended with her son and his parents told me I am a guardian angel. I am the blessing that wasn't appreciated. I will always love you both and appreciate God's blessings. God called her home in September of 2016. "To know her was to love her." Granddaddy was so delighted when he and Joshua have movie or dinner dates with each other. Sometimes they watch football games together. Granddaddy loves spoiling his grandson. Both look forward to sharing this joy with one another. In their family tradition, birthdays are celebrated every year. All would sit around the table have dinner, eat cake and ice cream, read cards, and open gifts. What a joyous time together!

Joshua loves grandma Robin's fried chicken! If he could, he will eat the whole pan. Grandma Robin also transports him to and from school daily, the Barber shop, along with the YMCA. Joshua likes going grocery shopping with his grandma Robin. These two will sit on the front steps or in the back yard enjoying the fresh air together. Grandma Robin loves Joshua very much, spoils him, and wants the best for her grandchild.

I thank God for the great support system he has given concerning Joshua. His aunts Carolyn and Sarah transport to ball games, school, shopping, and spend weekends together. Joshua looks forward to spending time with his cousin Keith, Sarah's son, going to the mall, Dave and Busters, ball games, haircuts, etc. We all encourage Joshua to do his best in school along with making the right choices in life. Sarah and Carolyn love

Joshua and he is dear to their hearts.

According to Joshua, it doesn't feel different being raised by a blind mother. I do everything a normal child would do. My life is extraordinary as I still take trips and partake in enjoyable activities. I have, and will always make sure my "baby" does everything he wants to do. He played basketball, football, baseball, track and field, cub scouts, wrestling, and bowled on a bowling league for 8 years. Once the bowling league ended for the year, a banquet was given and children received trophies, patches, and a certificate that displayed their game average. Cubs had a spaghetti dinner where the kids got pins and awards. All other sports mentioned gave trophies with certificates to celebrate their wins, annually. Every year for his birthday we celebrated for 3 days in a row. Cupcakes, pizza and drinks are taken to the school for he and his class mates. He's had parties at Chuckie Cheese, ice skating/roller skating, bowling, laser tag, party bus which allows children to play a variety of video games for a certain amount of time. One year he spent the weekend with family and friends at the Great Wolf Lodge in Williamsburg Virginia. Birthday child received an unlimited ice cream, cake, swim, or ride the rides that were in the park. It was a fantastic weekend filled with fun, love and joy. God blessed me with my precious gift just as he says in James 1: 17: "Every good and perfect gift is from above."

Recently in 2017, Joshua got involved with a mentoring program. Here at the program, the youth between the ages of 8 years old and 18 are taught to be effective positive leaders. Within 7 months of being in the program, my son has received a certificate in (CPR), Cardio Pulmonary Recessitation. They learned how to administer Narcan, which is a medication given to someone to treat an overdose of heroin or pain killers. They also learned how to pack a wound using a shoe string or shirt is a person is injured awaiting the paramedics.

People will say my child doesn't need that program, that's for bad children. That what's wrong with society. Stigma has been placed on things such as mentoring programs or psychiatrists. If your child does need help, they aren't able to obtain it because you feel the child shouldn't get it. Sometimes we have to take a step back and realize there are things put in place to keep our children out of the criminal system, assist with summer jobs, train the minors in Cyber security so once they complete high school they are able to encounter employment.

Kids can benefit from mentoring programs like these because people are there to become role models particularly when there is an absent parent. The mentoring program offers math and reading tutoring two times a week, field trips, talent shows, each child goes to the YMCA the first Saturday of the month to swim, have weight training, cardio, or basketball. Other trips included the U.S. Naval Base, Ground Zero, Time Square, the Soul Circus, Washington Wizard games in D C, Oriole baseball games, along with Madison Square Garden Stadium. Parents, children and the staff at the mentoring program received a presentation from the president, tour as well as a t-shirt. They have brought in a variety of speakers that includes judges, lawyers, basketball coaches, prison staff, and school principals. The speakers shed light on their positions to give insight to the youth for future employment opportunities. The director wants them to see that they have a future. Life is not about the street, gangs, violence or criminal system. He also believes that education is important.

Mentoring programs generate a scholarship for $1,000 to every child who are accepted into a college or some type of trade school. I think this is a magnificent help to our children. If we, as parents, could start viewing things with another approach and see the benefit, not looking at them as a stigmatism, I guarantee your youngsters will profit in the long run. It becomes a major problem when our babies aren't exposed to such platforms. The young kids and the staff of Mentoring program took a trip to Syracuse New York over the weekend. I was a little apprehensive about letting my child go on the trip. Reason is that he's never been on a trip without me nor a family member. I didn't want my young king to be surrounded by peers that would have a negative influence on him. Staff assured me everything was going to be alright. They told me not to worry. We made a joke that I would turn up for the weekend. I am so glad I decided to allow Joshua to experience such an event. All staff and kids toured Syracuse University as they acquired the admissions process concerning the educational institution. They ate at a buffet, a pizza party, toured the dome where Carmelo Anthony played basketball. A boat Cruise down Skaneateles Lake, granted a tour through the town of New York. Chaperones along with the children experienced a wonderful time as Joshua got freedom away from his mother. This was an opportunity to see if he could be responsible to be without me, being on his best behavior. He behaved well. God kept them all under His ark of safety.

Many conventions were held on the state/national level concerning the National Federation for the Blind around the globe. My son and I attend every year. Conventions are a way to network with sighted and non-sighted peers, pass resolutions, while viewing updated assistive technology for the blind. Joshua enjoys taking the blind to and from meetings, restaurants, or hotel rooms. He really loves helping them just as much as selling candy or portable phone chargers to raise money per the National Federation for the Blind Institute.

Joshua has a sibling named Jordan on his father side. Her mother and I agree that we would share because she knew that Jordan is like the daughter I never had. I always treated her just like she was my own. Jordan gave Joshua his name. Why? There was a little boy in her class that she liked and that's how her little brother got his name. Joshua and Jordan are very close. Jordan and her brother communicate daily. They enjoy their brother and sister time together. Those two are always planning something: movies, dinners, going to the mall, even if it's just to drive around sight see and talk with one another. We the parents, grandparents, and aunt made sure the kids attended family functions and traveled out of town. Boy, did we have a blast!!!! Nothing will be able to separate those two, the love they have for each other, they have a bond that will never be broken.

Until you really get to know a person, you cannot judge what you hear about a person and become a part of them. A good example is Clarence and Tracy. A husband and wife that are 2 peas in a pod. These two are blind and run their own household. They love people, love to entertain, love comedians, and if you ever been to one of their gatherings and you left hungry, it was all on you. They are full of laughter and a joy to be around.

I met the couple at the Washington seminar. Tracy was my mentor. Beyond mentoring they became my adopted parents (parents away from home.) They are one of my biggest supporters when it comes to making decisions in my life. I thought it was a wise choice to ask them to be my son's God parents.

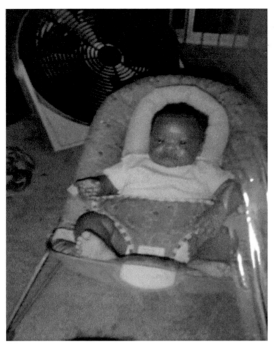

* (Joshua as a baby)

* (Joshua, Jordan, and I)

* (Joshua and Bob)

* (Joshua and his grandfather Dawn)

My Experience with The National Federation of the Blind and Maryland's Governor

27 years ago, I started working with the President and the National Federation of the Blind on both the national and state level. In addition to my various leadership roles on the Student Division board, and willingness to help in any capacity, I spent a great deal of time assisting with the NFB's legislative agenda. As many of the bills we fought to pass directly improve my life, I endeavored to assist in any way that I could. I helped to write letters, attend hearings, and present information on our proposed bills in the presence of state Senators and Delegates as well as national Congressmen and Senators. Several bills that I worked on to pass include the Space Available Act for disabled Veterans, the Pedestrian Safety Act requiring all quiet cars to omit an audible noise when idling, and the efforts to end the segregated ballot system plaguing blind voters in Maryland.

Most recently, I helped to get the Marrakesh treaty passed. The Marrakesh S259, implementing act of the treaty would allow the blind to have access to thousands of books in an alternative format. These formats include Braille, CD, audible, or a PDF file. After successfully lobbying efforts culminating with the passage of the bill, blind individuals now have the same access to a variety of books as their sighted peers all over the world including the United States.

As a parent, I felt especially drawn protecting the rights of blind parents in Maryland. The parental Rights Bill SB765 and HB976 preserve the right of blind parents to care for their biological children, adoption, receiving a child through foster care, and taking guardianship of a child. Blind parents should not have to face unfair preconceived biases from society along with negative attitudes concerning the ability to parent their children. The opposition's reasons stem from family and dependency law proceedings where custody and visitation are at stake and in public and private adoption, guardianship and foster care proceedings. As a result, children are being removed from their parent's home and their children are not able to enjoy time with their families due to restriction per family court. Signing this bill into law provides a safety net to blind parents or caretakers because they are able to demonstrate to society and the family court that the visually impaired are capable of caring for their children.

Parents also have the opportunity to implement supportive parenting services to alleviate concerns that have been raised. Family court may require these services be put in place and reviewed if needed at any time. In a case where parent's rights are denied in custody, visitation, foster care, adoption, or guardianship, the court is to write specific findings stating the basis for the determination and why the provision of parent supportive services is not a reasonable accommodation that must be made to prevent the denial or limitation. Having the opportunity to testify in a hearing before the senate not only allowed me to share my experiences and expertise in reference to parenting a child as a blind parent spoke to the need that the parental rights bill needed to be passed and sign into law immediately.

My legislative efforts spanned beyond the NFB community as I also had the opportunity to work on a committee appointed by Maryland's Governor. As a member of the Personal Assistance Service Advisory and standardize training Committee, I helped to propose a budget and make recommendations to the governor concerning how medical care for the elderly should be render. We also advised him on matters concerning pay rates for Certified Nursing Assistants/Geriatric Nursing Assistants (CNA/GNA,). I also had the chance to participate in discussions concerning disability rights. I believe blindness is not what holds one back; rather it is the obstacle that stands in one's way.

3

DEPRESSION AND SETBACKS

Later in adulthood, I was employed in a variety of occupations. I managed and operated a full- service cafeteria. As the manager of the cafeteria, menus were planned daily, weekly bank deposits made, assigned duties were given to staff, the manager ran the register, and inventory was done daily. Five employees were supervised by me. I was employed at a beauty salon. Appointments were scheduled, and calls were transferred to the appropriate hair stylist. I was an usher at Harbor Park Movie Theater and her duties included directing patrons to movie theaters, collecting tickets and maintaining cleanliness of restrooms and theaters.

Maryland School for the Blind hired me as a switch Board Operator where calls was transferred to appropriate person or department. Another position that I held there was a Childcare Assistant. I assisted with recess, circle time where children learned days of the week, months on the calendar, numbers, and ABC'. I also assisted with story time, arts and crafts, prepared breakfast and lunch for children, and helped with dismissal at the end of day.

For 9 years, I worked as a contact representative in the federal government where I answered inquiries from the public concerning, Social Security Disability Insurance, Supplemental Security Income, Retirement, Medicare/Medicaid, set up and cancelled direct deposits, updated addresses, and referred clients to appropriate offices. These included Department of Social Services, Eviction Prevention, Railroad Retirement Board, Financial Aid, Veterans Administration, and Internal Revenue Service. Other duties included mailing benefit verification letters, 1099's, replacement social security cards, medicare cards, claims for Supplemental Security Income, Social Security Disability Insurance, Retirement, Widows benefits, Survivors Benefits, and sent messages via field office or payment center. There were times when I dealt with crisis responses from the public, a written report was taken, and followed proper procedures. Unfortunately, I was unable to perform my duties as a Tele-Service Representative due to debilitating health conditions as well as an injury that occurred on the job.

On January 9, 2014 I, arrived at work at approximately 8:30 A.M. I am a totally blind individual who sustained multiple injuries around 9:35 that morning at the Federal Government agency. I tripped and fell over a wooden palette while walking to the front of my unit to give my supervisor reasonable accommodation forms. The wooden Palette was on the 3rd floor, in the front of the unit, in the middle of the isle.

As I fell, I landed on both arms, hit my right foot, knee, injured both arms and hands, and elbows. Immediately after the injury occurred, I felt excruciating pain in foot, knee, elbows, arms, and hands, along with tingling and numbness. There was also swelling in right knee and foot as well as a tremendous amount of pain in neck and back 24 hours after the trauma occurred.

While experiencing these symptoms on January 9th 2014, I sought medical treatment from the Health Suite at the federal government. The nurse placed an ice pack on swollen knee and informed me to contact my supervisor and have him bring workers comp documents to the health suite so that I could take them to physician to be completed once medical treatment was rendered. My supervisor was also advised to complete a portion of the workers comp form, per federal government's Medical staff.

Once paperwork was brought to health suite, around 11:30 A.M., I was transported to the Hospital in a taxi cab to seek further medical treatment. Hospital's medical Staff provided medication; X-rays, finalized worker's comp forms, and instructed me to follow up with primary care physician within 2 to 4 days.

I followed up with my Primary Care Physician on January 13th 2014. As a concerned Medical Practitioner, my doctor ordered physical therapy, medication, and submitted documentation to be out of work from the time the injury occurred, which was January 9th 2014 and return to work on January 28th 2014. There were no other previous injuries at the time of the fall.

Currently I suffer from several disabilities, as well as the Worker's Compensation injuries that were sustained on the job, in January of 2014. The Worker's Compensation injuries included: an upper sprain to my neck, contusion to right knee and shoulder region, back pain, enlarged disc in back; and hip, knee, and foot pain.

I suffer from tenosynovitis (tendonitis) and the symptoms are that I experience stems from swelling in the muscles, arms, wrists, and hand; tenderness, inflammation, excruciating pain, along with difficulty moving specific joints necessary for repetitive typing, which is a part of my daily work duties. I was diagnosed with this condition which was caused by repetitive typing on the job. However, after sustaining multiple injuries as a result of tripping over the wooden pallets that were left in the middle of the aisle (walkway), in the unit where I am currently employed, my condition of tendonitis has worsened.

Another condition that affects my health is neuropathy in my hands and fingers. Neuropathy affects one or more peripheral nerves that cause numbness and weakness. This condition developed and is also exacerbated by repetitive typing on the job. The combination of the injuries due to the fall I had while at work and the injuries from repetitive typing cause me to experience numbness, tingling, muscle weakness, excruciating pain, sleep interference, and sensitivity to touch.

Finally, I suffer from hypermobility syndrome, Danlos Ehlers Syndrome, which is a genetic disorder that causes joint pain. Hypermobility syndrome is a condition that is detrimental to my health. It is a genetic disorder that involves chronic joint pain, muscle weakness, easy bruising, fatigue, and hypermobility in my joints, which causes my joints to move and become dislocated.

In conclusion, it is difficult for me to perform the duties of my current position as a Tele-service Representative because of these debilitating conditions. I am unable to sit or stand for long periods of time. I can type no more than 5 minutes before experiencing a tremendous amount of pain in my arms, hands, fingers, back, neck, and tingling in my hands and fingers. All conditions are being treated with sedating medications, gentle exercises, and physical therapy. Therefore, I decided to leave the agency after receiving disability retirement. I filed an EEO with an agency within the federal government concerning discrimination due to a disability, failure to promote, failure to provide reasonable accommodations, failure to process workers compensation claim, and harassment. I hired an attorney to represent my case. However I ended up representing myself after I was scammed out of $1,500. On the next page, you will find the complaint that I sent to the Bar Council along with the attorney's response.

To whom it may concern:

I am a totally blind individual and single parent of an eleven-year-old son. I am writing this letter to file a formal complaint with the Attorney Grievance Commission. On February 23, 2015, I signed a retainer agreement with Attorney Black, of G and G law firm, to represent me in an EEO case with an agency in the federal government concerning discrimination due to a disability, failure to promote, failure to provide reasonable accommodations, failure to process Workers Compensation claim, and harassment. Attorney Black charged me a fee of $1,500, which he said was a flat fee, which I paid as a debit from my credit card on February25, 2015.

After the agreement was signed and faxed to the law firm, a copy of the ROI report, as well as a CD of all documents, requested by the law firm, was mailed to Attorney Black to review. The copy of the CD, appeal rights, and the faxing of the retainer agreement cost a total of $31.00, also paid by me.

On March 2, 2015, I received an email from Ms. Green, an employee at the G and G Law Firm, who informed me that a hearing request was submitted. In April, I requested to have a meeting with Attorney Black and Ms. Green, via email, to discuss my EEO case. A meeting was scheduled for April 16, 2015 in Attorney Black office. During the meeting, Attorney Black recommended that the hearing be suspended, which I did not agree to do because I had applied and was approved for Federal Retirement Disability. Therefore, I did not want the hearing to be suspended due to the fact that the agency was liable for compensatory damages.

The Federal Retirement Disability case and the EEO case were two different issues. Attorney Black did not represent me in the Federal Disability for Retirement case; however, I faxed him the approval letter because I felt it was important for the attorney to know this information.

Attorney Black agreed that the agency was liable for some damages and requested me to send all of my medical records to his office so that compensatory damages could be sought from the agency. I had all of my records copied onto a CD and sent to his office, which cost me an additional $177.89.

On April 23, 2015, I requested a copy of the expense worksheet along with the status of my case. I received an email from Ms. Green stating "I don't know what hearing request you are referring to." "With regards to your retainer, your agreement states that it is a flat fee case. "There will be no additional discovery or filing charges." The initial payment of $1500 is not refundable. "We are working on other aspects of your case."

Another email was sent on May 22, 2015 concerning status of case. I didn't receive a response until I contacted MS. Green on May 26, 2015 via the telephone. Ms. Green informed me that they were in trial all week and she was working on the learning memorandum to suggest to the federal government's agency how to better work with disabled employees and that Attorney Black had referred the compensatory damage part of the case to another attorney." I asked Ms. Green who the other Attorney was. She replied, "Bamby asked me to give her until next week to get back to me and if I did not hear from her, to contact the law firm.

I contacted Ms. Green, via email, June 2, 2015 and did not receive a response. I also contacted Ms. Green via the telephone on June 2nd and June 3rd, without receiving a response until approximately 4:40 p.m. on June 3rd when I received an email from Ms. Green saying that I would be receiving a formal summary letter within 10 days.

This is the second time that I have had to file a complaint with the Attorney Grievance Commission. I am overwhelmed, stressed, and in disbelief because I have been not only being given false information from the attorney, but I have also been scammed out of $1500 plus additional expenses.

When I contacted the Federal Government on June 4, 2015 to see if Attorney Black has been in contact with them or if a hearing request had been made, I was informed that my attorney had not submitted the hearing request nor had he contacted the agency. Unfortunately, the agency has rendered a decision against me because of my attorney's lack of action and informed me that I will have to appeal my EEO case once I receive the decision in the mail.

I am requesting that all expenses and any compensatory damages that I would have won from my EEO case be paid to me by Mr. Black. If you have any questions, please contact me via email schoolyard@aol.com or (410) 555-1234.

Thank you,
Uniquelyblessed1

123 Main Street

Fallston, Maryland 21047

07/31/2015

To whom it may concern,

I am responding to the objections written by Attorney Black from G and G Law Firm. I feel that I was misrepresented, taking advantage of due to my blindness. I feel that my blindness led Mr. Black to believe I was incompetent based on my blindness and therefore, records were falsified. As a result, I was scammed out of $1500.

Mediation never took place and a settlement was never discussed or offered. However, I am no longer with the federal government because I applied for Disability Retirement myself without legal representation in May of 2014. I was approved for benefits around March 20th 2015. Mr. Black was retained on February 23rd 2015 to represent me in an EEO case with the federal government concerning discrimination due to disability, failure to promote, failure to provide reasonable accommodations, failure to process workers compensation claim, and harassment. Nevertheless, I informed Mr. Black of me getting approved for disability benefits because I felt that it was a crucial piece of information, even though it had nothing to do with retaining him as a lawyer. Mr. Black was retained to represent me in an EEO case against the federal government and not retained for Disability Retirement, which I handled myself. I was charged a retainer's fee in the amount of $1,500, which was taken out of my account on February 25th, 2015. I was never charged an additional$1,000 fee at all because discovery was not needed. My Disability Retirement Benefit was approved on March 20th, which clearly states that Mr. Black had nothing to do with that decision.

The attorneys are not being honest about stating that there was a hearing, no hearing was ever requested by Attorney Black or Green.

According to Attorney Black, He alleges that a hearing request was submitted on March 2, 2015. However, when I researched the tracking number 940021184956280137l243 on stamps.com as well as the postal service, no tracking number could be found.

On June 4th, 2015, I spoke with an employee who works in the Office of Civil Rights and Equal Opportunity who advised me that a hearing request was never submitted. This is a clear indication that Attorney Black's records were falsified, which further shows that I was never represented by Mr. Black's firm. I am also stating that the agency was not aware of me having legal representation because Mr. Black did not submit the designee form, yet he debited my card in the amount of $1,500 and I received no legal services from this firm. Instead, I had to take it upon myself to send in the designee representation form, which states Mr. Black was my lawyer as of 04/16/2015.

Ms. Green emailed a learning Memorandum that I requested to be mailed to the Commissioner of the agency, however this does not constitute $1,500 of retainer fees.

After the agreement was signed and faxed to the law firm, a copy of the Report of Investigations, (ROI) , as well as a CD of all documents, requested by the law firm, was mailed to Attorney Black to review. The copy of the CD, appeal rights, and the faxing of the retainer agreement cost a total of $31.00, also paid by me.

On March 2, 2015, I received an email from Ms. Green, an employee at the G and G Law Firm, who informed me that a hearing request was submitted. Attorney Black alleges that a final conference took place on April 16 2015. In April, I requested to have a meeting with Attorney Black and Ms. Green, via email, to discuss my EEO case. A meeting was scheduled for April 16, 2015 in Attorney Black's office. During the meeting, Attorney Black recommended that the hearing be suspended, which I did not agree to do because I had applied and was approved for Federal Retirement Disability. Therefore, I did not want the hearing to be suspended due to the fact that the agency was liable for compensatory damages.

Attorney Black agreed that the agency was liable for some damages and requested me to send all of my medical records to his office so that compensatory damages could be sought from the agency within the federal government. I had all of my records copied onto a CD and sent to his office, which cost me an additional $177.89.

On April 23, 2015, I requested a copy of the expense worksheet along with the status of my case. I received an email from Ms. Green stating "I don't know what hearing request you are referring to." "With regards to your retainer, your agreement states that it is a flat fee case. "There will be no additional discovery or filing charges." The initial payment of $1500 is a flat fee. There will be no additional filing fees. "The initial fee of $1500 is not refundable." "We are working on other aspects of your case."

Another email was sent on May 22, 2015 concerning status of case. I didn't receive a response until I contacted MS. Green on May 26, 2015 via the telephone. Ms. Green informed me that they were in trial all week and she was working on the learning memorandum to suggest to the agency how to better work with disabled employees and that Attorney Black had referred the compensatory damage part of the case to another attorney." I asked Ms. Green who the other Attorney was. She replied, "Bamby." Ms. Green asked me to give her until next week to get back to me and if I did not hear from her, to contact the law firm.

I contacted Ms. Green, via email, June 2, 2015 and did not receive a response. I also contacted Ms. Green via the telephone on June 2nd and June 3rd, without receiving a response until approximately 4:40 p.m. on June 3rd when I received an email from Ms. Green saying that I would be receiving a formal summary letter within 10 days. I never received a formal summary letter from Ms. Green.

On June 23rd I requested the status of my case via email. Ms. Green didn't respond until June 24, 2015 stating that "my case has concluded when I accepted early retirement. "Therefore, we are no longer working on that case." I was not aware of my case being closed until after receiving email mentioned above.

I am overwhelmed, stressed, and in disbelief because I have not only been given false information from the attorney, but I have also been scammed out of $1500 plus additional expenses.

In conclusion, attorney Black misrepresented me due to my blindness. I was taken advantage of because of my disability. I do not feel it was no other reason but my blindness.

Having an attorney take cold advantage of a person with a disability makes you not want to trust anyone. All kinds of feelings ran through my head as a result of being overwhelmed with a hostile work environment, harassment on a daily basis, not to mention now that your attorney allegedly was supposed to represent you has now ripped you off. I was furious, had to pray, shed tears, and communicate with my pastor. After much prayer, I decided to represent myself and settled out of court and take the measly settlement that was offered. God is good! Prayer works, although the attorney didn't apologize nor did he accept the fact that he's wrong. He doesn't have to answer to me but to the Lord. God's word tells us in James 5:16 to "confess your fault one to another and pray one for another that you may be healed". Also the same scripture continues: " the effectual fervent prayer of the righteous man availeth much." Going into disability retirement was a difficult decision to make. I felt like I lost my sense of independence. I tried going back to work but was unable to perform the duties at hand the at the time due to multiple setbacks: my blindness, multiple injuries while employed, n and being diagnosed with a genetic disorder, which changed my whole world. I had to remember to hold on to my faith because I can't fight these battles on my own. I had to let God fight the battles for me! However, after years of therapy I am able to refocus so that I can concentrate on goals. Although I have not medically recovered, therapy is an opportunity to hit the reset button due to talking to someone about these issues you're faced with and now I can move forward.

4

THERAPY SUITS MY CASE

Depression is a chemical imbalance in the brain. These chemicals are call dopamine and serotonin. Such chemicals affect the ability to feel pleasure or wellbeing which cause depression if the brain doesn't make enough or its not processing correctly. Various symptoms of depression are anxiety, anger, feeling hopeless or worthless, difficulty enjoying activities one use to like, changes in weight or eating habits. Others include getting to much or too little sleep, crying, sadness, thoughts of suicide, or unexplained physical ailment such as headaches or muscle pain. Anger, shame and irritation are felt when people suffer from depression. These emotions will show in the body as nausea or aches. People may feel numb as if they have no energy. With severe cases, you don't care if you live or die. According to goodtherapy.org, one in 10 individuals experience depression and they will have an episode in their late teens or early twenties.

Often depression is found more in women than men. Men don't want to discuss their feelings or problems. It makes them feel weak or less of a man. As a result, therapy is avoided. Men who suffer from depression exemplify symptoms that includes anger, difficulty sleeping, or become fatigued. They cope by escaping behaviors that involve sexual affairs and binge drinking. Women who experience depression have symptoms such as   loss of appetite, fatigue, difficulty sleeping, crying, sadness, mood changes, attempting suicide, they also experience premenstrual dysphoria (PMDD.) This occurs when severe depression takes place before a woman's period but symptoms will improve once period has started. They may disappear for the rest of the cycle.

Around 2 percent of children between the ages of 6 and 12 years old experience some type of depression. It is about 7% for teenagers. According to statistics, 60% of youth who suffer are not seeking therapy. Some children may inherit abnormalities in brain chemistry from parents. Therefore, kids are more LIKELY to share their parent's depression. If the adult's depression affects their parenting, the child learns certain behavior and attitudes. Depression maybe developed as a response to stress.

Depression not only affects the individual but it also affects the loved ones of that particular person. Supporting these individuals can be very difficult due to claiming they don't deserve love so comfort is not accepted per goodtherapy.org. As a result, you see irritability which put strain on the relationship. Love ones become frustrated as well as confused when their support doesn't cure loved one's depression.

Poem I

I was that individual dealing with depression.

Having family, clergy, and friends on my behalf make intercession.

From losing loved ones, dealing with situations and bad relationships that impact your life,

Even sustaining multiple injuries on the job while maintaining

Families hating, not anticipating family strife.

  Baby daddy cheating, telling me don't worry, the relationship will work out without a doubt.

Then in the same breath told me,

There is someone else you see.

Boo don't be a fool.

Heal, go out and get a new tool.

Bought him a car thinking we wouldn't have to pay transportation to travel so far.

Allegedly afraid to stay informing neighbors/ friends that our son would fall off of the bed as I was falsely accused.

All along that was his excuse to go out and play, instead I was verbally abused and used,

Scorn, talked about just as sure as I was born.

Kept his other son from being removed from the home, but he acts like I was his thorn,

Pampers, bottles, tea shirts, blankets I was there to provide,

Used my van to store belongings in my home, help I tried.

Raising a child to the best of my ability yet went through financial instability.

Hearing things like child would fall off the bed is a comedy.

Yet I'm the one with full custody.

Years later apologized as he swallowed pride,

I forgave as God is my guide.

Therapy Suit my Case

Poem II

Someone who was God -fearing, and close to my heart always told me

To achieve my goals and dreams

Always strive to do your best, as you climb to reach the top

He made sure that I knew that he knew that I was beautiful, and sexy

I felt Adoration as he gazed in my beautiful eyes

A man whose intelligent, yet diligent

He decided to drive as a form of relaxation being vigilant

My first love is a victim of gun violence

One who went home as I waited for his call after enjoying time together

As It felt like silence.

Hurt pain, I just can't explain…

Depression is not a game

If you need help don't be ashamed

Feeling anger, anxiety sadness, loss of appetite, mood change or irritation

Pray to God as you sit in meditation

Being able to vent, discuss problems privately in a space

With a mental health clinician

Cognitive, psychodynamic, and psycho education therapy suits my case

5

KNOW YOUR WORTH

Story I

Dating the Blind Pimp

The man that I avoided for a long time was finally given a chance. Mike was married and he knew that I would not date someone who is married. He fabricated the story by telling me that he was divorced and we went out to dinner.

I went on judiciary case search to see if Mike was divorced and there weren't any record with data saying he and his wife were divorced. We went out on a couple of dates. I attended a party and 3 women were there that he was dating and neither one knew each other. We all thought we were his significant other. All along Mike was never divorced just separated. His wife still had a key to the house and could enter anytime she pleased. There many times I had to leave because the wife was coming over. I would come back after she was gone. Mike was arrogant, rude and disrespectful. He wasn't over his wife. One day I spent the night with him and he decided that I would sleep on the couch while he and another female were having sex in his room. Mike thought I was a fool when I began to question him concerning the female. I heard them having sex and this was disgusting and a disgrace. He tried to tell me that it was the female and his cousin in his room. That was a lie, I heard both of them going up the stairs as he tried to sneak and do it. I felt stupid, asking myself how did I get myself in a situation like this? Every time I tried to leave him alone, he begged me to stay. Instead, I should have left. He used the woman and sex as scapegoats to fill the empty void which was his wife. He reminded me of a male prostitute as it relate to the female prostitute Rahab found in scripture, Joshua 2.

Another incident occurred when Mike and I decided to spend quality time together. Of course a woman had to be involved I was sleep in the bed and Mike planned to put me on the couch again to bring his fling to the room. That didn't happen. I gave him a piece of my mind and started putting my shoes on to call a cab to go home. I never realized it was after 2 in the morning. I told him I don't care what you do. I'm staying in this bed and he and the girl stayed on the couch downstairs. He didn't want me to leave that time of morning by myself. You would think this was my breaking point.

Mike and his wife had 2 children, a boy and girl. My son played with them from time to time. The straw that broke the camel's back in this relationship was when Trina, Mike, a friend and I, all went out. Mike began talking to my friend Tanya who was with us as he tried to get involved in a relationship with her. His bubble was busted. Tanya explained that she was a loyal friend to me and you don't do friends like that. She also explained that she doesn't talk to men that her involved with her friends. Mike denied our relationship, thinking that Tanya would fall for it.

72

However, it didn't work.

I began praying to God asking if he get me out of this situation, I promise I will never get in another again. When we broke up, I would ask Mike if Joshua could see his 2 children. Mike told me he had to ask the children if it was ok as if he needed permission from them. I explained to my son that people hurt people. We have to pray for them. Sometimes you have to let who you thought were your friends go and find new ones. This is a relationship that I should have continued to avoid. I wish I never opened this particular chapter at all. But when a woman is fed up Ain't nothing you can do about it. God always provides a way out. 1 Corinthians 10: 13, "No temptation has seized you except what is common to man. And God is faithful. He will not let you be tempted beyond what you can bear But when you are tempted, He will provide an escape so that you can stand up under it".

Story II

Dating Charles

I started dating this guy with a huge house out of state. The house had 8 bedrooms, 5 bathrooms and large backyard. This man talked a good game and I fell in to his trap until I saw the real person. I needed a place to stay for 3 weeks until my son graduated from elementary school. He made excuses and said my son and I could not reside there. He said "I'll help you find a hotel. He didn't help pay for it. However, he brought food for my son and me to eat. I guess that was his way of showing he cared and being a jerk at the same time. I couldn't believe he would allow someone to come to an unfamiliar state where they didn't know anything about, but instead of allowing us to reside at his place; he rather see me stranded with a minor child struggling to find money to pay for a hotel.

Charles mistreated my son, such as beating him with a belt because he didn't fold a blanket; telling him spread his legs like a criminal. I became furious and ran over to get my child. I carried him for 9 months and I'm not going to allow anyone to treat no child, especially my own, in that manner. Joshua didn't know anything about spreading your legs like a criminal. Once I made sure my child was alright, I gave him a piece of my mind and that never happened again. Never-the-less, he didn't raise his own children but had the nerve to tell somebody else how to raise theirs. Let's not forget he always belittled me, saying things like you are a piss poor parent, you're not wife material, Sex isn't good and can't feel the walls etc. etc. The devil is a liar! I am an excellent parent who has done nothing but the best when raising my son, as a single parent. I would never let anyone try to change my mind nor make me think differently. I told him If you don't appreciate me for who I am, someone else will appreciate an excellent wife.

He played the game of acting as if he wanted to marry me. He asked me to set up counseling sessions with my pastor. We had counseling sessions several times via the phone. But he was to attend one session in person and that didn't happen. Every time my pastor asked if we had a marriage date, Charles was unable to answer. Eventually I canceled the sessions because I felt it was a waste of time and I wanted Pastor to give his time to a couple that was serious about getting married and not playing games. A stupid statement came from his mouth, "Why did you cancel? I wanted us to have those sessions to prepare and show you how to be a good wife." We even read the book that my Pastor recommended called Marriage for Women, Marriage for Men only by Tony Evans. The man said I sabotaged him when we were in session with my Pastor. This blew Pastor away. Pastor couldn't believe he said such a thing. Pastor asked Charles why would she do something like that? That's not in her character. Charles hesitated. Pastor and I agree that he was not the right one. This same man tried to seduce one of my relatives. I guess he thought I would never find that out. He was sadly mistaken. The signs were there. I should have left him a long time ago.

One year, the guy, my son, and I went to a convention out of town. I reimbursed him for the hotel stay. During the convention he was very disrespectful. He acted as if I wasn't present. He went on dates with other women and at times, walked past me without speaking to me. My friends along with my child saw him with these other women. It was told to the women that he bought us to the convention because we needed a place to stay for a while because I was homeless. Of course, this was false. Charles wanted to have his cake and eat it too. That was not going to happen with me. I have a 3-bedroom home, two bathrooms, and a nice backyard. The front was nice. My house was cute, it was the right size for my son and myself. I brought Christmas and birthday gifts. He received an edible arrangements for his birthday and he told me "that shit was nasty." "I don't want it." The outfit that was purchased for Christmas was never accepted from post office and eventually it was mailed back to me. His response was "I don't accept giftsteay from my girlfriend or friend, only if you are my wife." I was disappointed. Charles was ungrateful. I have never encountered a person like him in my life. Being the significant other to someone who didn't appreciate me at all when all I did was help in whatever way I could. I also assisted with paperwork when he needed advice with disability benefits. My family was so upset with the way he treated me. My dad never wanted to see him again because you don't hurt daddy's little girl. When I have done the best that I could and it is not appreciated, I have to move on and count my blessing because I'm better than that and I deserve so much more.

Story III

Dating Ted

One day during the summer when my son's football game had ended, transportation came to pick us up. Once we boarded the vehicle, the gentleman and I had an interesting conversation concerning relationships. The driver, Ted, was interested in me and we exchanged numbers. He told me to contact him after he got off work that night. I said this man is crazy and has lost his mind. I agreed to contact him. I thought he was everything and a bag of chips. He was a handsome, bald head, sexy chocolate man; the apple of my eye, everything I had been searching for.

We began to date and he became the love of my life. I knew he was the one who I was to marry. My family really liked him and they thought the same. I packed all of my things and we decided that I should move in his apartment and become one family. This was out of my character. Normally I would not do such a thing. Both of our names had to be on the lease or mortgage deed before I would even think about doing something like reside with a man. I thought I was in love with the man of my dreams. This is the one, so I thought! Joshua loved him and started calling him dad after permission was granted from both adults. He started calling Joshua his son and everyone began claiming one another. Ted is a great father to his children and Joshua. He loved him, unconditionally, and would do anything to insure that their needs are met. His family met us and starting coming to Joshua's ball games. Joshua appreciated it. This meant a lot to my son because he was looking for that male role model, which was a father figure in his life.

After meeting his family, I knew this relationship was going to work. They were so receptive to me being blind and his mom Kate loved us. Kate accepted my son as her grandchild. Ted has 5 children and all are girls. They are Winter, Summer, Tuesday, Thursday, and September. Ted raised 4 of his children and the oldest child resides with her mother. We all loved one another. Every Sunday, the family went to church, came home, had dinner watched movies, laughed and joked before going to bed. We played games too.

One of Ted's children, Tuesday was going to be baptized but she was afraid. Ted and I consoled her and let her know that it was ok. It's always the next time. We gave her hugs and kisses and enjoyed the rest of the service as a family. Winter his second oldest daughter loved the church and wanted to continue going. I encouraged her to do so. Every night the family and I prayed before going to bed. Often, the family would visit my mother's house to dine with her and the rest of my family. Before going to bed I would give each one a hug, kiss and tell them I love you including my son. They replied the same. The relationship happened so fast like a movie that flashed before my eyes.

Ted and I discussed moving out of town after my home was sold. We were looking at moving to North Carolina. Before I met Ted, I planned to move out of state to give my child a different atmosphere as well as a better education. There's a lot of crime and the public schools in Baltimore area not the greatest. We also viewed the option of living in Georgia due to the fact that my son and I loved it there. I thought they had the best educational system in the world. My son did exceptionally well while attending school in Georgia. He graduated with the highest average in English, Math, and Social Studies. Joshua never caught the bus until he asked Ted and myself if he could learn how to catch the bus to school. Winter agreed to teach him. That was one of the best times in his life! His big sister showed him how to get to school on an MTA bus. As a single parent, I am over protective and don't want anything to happen to my baby. I was afraid to have him catch the bus. I realized I had to let go and allow my faith and God take control. I always prayed, asked God to keep my baby safe and He always does. God's word speaks of keeping our offspring secure in Psalms 102:28 because it says, " The children of your servant shall dwell secure. Their offspring shall be established before you.

I loved Ted's children just like they were my own. When I purchased gifts for Christmas and for Joshua's birthday, I purchased gifts for Ted's children as well. I planned a birthday party and wedding proposal for Ted. It was a surprise and his family were so excited. Winter said, "This will be the best birthday ever for him." Both families were there and we had all kinds of food, a huge pretty cake, and I sang to him as I proposed. I know this is out of the norm. However, a wedding proposal was something I always wanted to do especially, if it was someone I loved and we both wanted to spend the rest of our lives together. I never wanted the traditional proposal, I wanted to be different. After the family shed tears, he said, " yes" to the proposal. Ted was in shock but happy. We took lots of pictures and I was the talk of the town.

For a while the relationship went great. We had disagreements and we were able to work them out. I thought everything was on track. A couple of days passed and Ted contacted me stating that the rental office found out about me and my child living there and he would be evicted if I didn't move. I was hurt and confused because I couldn't understand why he couldn't just put me on the lease. I began to pack my stuff as I tried to figure where I was going to go because I already sold my house. Lesson learned always keep your own place or demand to be on the lease or mortgage deed. I found out later on that the story concerning the eviction was a ploy to get me out of the house. After I kept questioning him, he decided he didn't want to be in the relationship any longer. That night was the worst night ever. I cried all night. I felt as if my whole world had been crushed. Emotions were all over the place. My heart was torn in pieces. This man was the man of my dreams. The one that I've been waiting for. But only to find out, "I was not the one that he wanted." He spoiled me. He made me feel like no other man has ever made me feel sexually, emotionally, or physically. This feeling was indescribable and unexplainable. He always gave a listening ear when needed like when my father died. When he needed a hand, I was there for him, too. We appreciated and loved each other. The game of psychology was played real well.

Allegedly we were supposed to go out on dates. We had an intense conversation one day that was engaging to both of us. The plan was to meet after work on a Friday evening. I wanted to see where things would go, if anywhere. He agreed to do so. Excuses came up. For instance, I get off late, I have an event in DC, I have a friend that I'm interested in, what did you think was going to happen, no babysitter for the girls. Instead of being honest and up front and saying he didn't want to meet or he wasn't interested; he played a lot of games; made all kinds of excuses. Ted gave me false hopes and I was hurt and disappointed. Men make time for what they want. This relationship is difficult for me to get over. I'm always thinking about this individual constantly no matter what. I cannot get this man out of my head. You can't help who you love. Love make you do some crazy things.

There have been several instances when his mom was ill. Medical treatment was sought. Out of concern, I wanted to see her but that was unsuccessful. I always inquired about the children, give updates when schools are delayed, or closed, send birthday messages, etc. I even asked to see the children because I gotten attached to them and they are my babies. Of course, that didn't happen until Winter brought them to see me recently. I was asked when we were together if anything ever happens to him, make sure his children are taken care of. Even though we are not in a relationship anymore, I took that commitment seriously and I will always honor it. Some people would say she's stupid or crazy. No, I'm just unique in my own way. In Psalms 139: 14 "I will praise You for I am fearfully and wonderfully made. Marvelous are your works and that my soul knows very well." I am blessed by the best. No matter what experiences I go through at that moment I know God is aware of all my needs.

God is always present, aware of my problems and needs. I was created in his likeness. God created me in his own design. I was created to do his good works. I was created to care for others. I can't afford not to give my God praise! He's done so many marvelous things in my life. There is none like him and God is greatly to be praised. The children didn't ask to come in this world and they didn't ask to be without motherly guidance. I the Christian person that I am will always inquire about them and pray for them. I will do whatever I can for those babies. In my opinion, I believe if Ted feels that someone is getting close to his children, he'll do anything to break the bond apart. Especially, if he doesn't want anything else to do with the person as far as a relationship is concerned. After we broke up, the family and I agreed to stay in contact with each other. Sometimes I wanted to speak with Winter and his mom. He informed me that their numbers have been changed. Winter number remained the same. Winter and I communicated via Facebook.

The crazy part about this whole thing is that I love this man who has the potential to be an excellent spouse, nice, yet so cold. He'll forever have a special place in my heart. I was not appreciated. Women know your worth. Don't settle for anything less than what you are worth. Men will do what you allow them to do. "Men will tell you what they want you to hear because they know that those things that are said will make the woman feel good. A lot of times you won't receive the truth from men because they don't want to hurt your feelings even though you're asking them to be honest. Ladies don't beat yourself up. Don't wonder if I would have done this, maybe things would had been different. Am I not good enough? Queens, we have to remember that you deserve more, you are royalty. Stand strong, stick your chest out and tell yourself, " I am somebody." Know that you are "More than a conqueror through Jesus Christ." According to Psalms 37:4 states "Delight yourself in the Lord and He will give you the desires of your heart." So, go to God in prayer, be specific and let him know what you are desiring in a help mate. Go boldly before the Lord and tell him what you want. If it's a man that's equally yoked, someone who can lift you up when you're torn and strengthen you when you're weak. Make it known to the Lord and he'll grant the desires of your heart in his own timing.

Be still and wait on God to bless you. Remember what we want may not always be good for us. God's word also tells us in Psalms 5:3 that God hears your voice as you bring your request to the Lord but we have to wait in expectation. While waiting, you know it's going to happen! You just don't know when or who your help mate will be. That's hard to do because we want what we want when we want it. We must learn to wait on God and know that God will bless us with that man that will love us, unconditionally. He will pour out his heart, love you more than you love him!!! He will chase after you. You will not have to chase him because you will be on his lips every second, every moment, and every hour, 365 days a year. Patience is a virtue. Proverbs 18: 22, " He who finds a wife, finds a good thing and obtains favor from the Lord

Winter and I have an excellent relationship. She told me that I was like a mother figure to her and she will always love and respect me. I will always love Winter like she is my own. She will always be another daughter I never had. Whenever she needs a listening ear or a shoulder to cry on, I am here for her. If she needs monetary assistance, I am here. " I do not take it lightly and count it as a privilege and an honor to be the woman you feel you can ask for help, support, or advice. But I will never try to take the place of your biological mother. My love for you will never change! Our bond will never be broken."

Sincere and I were best friends since the age of 5 years old. My mom and best friend sister Kellyanne were really good friends. Kellyanne used to watch my sister Sarah and I when my mother worked in the field of nursing. Many times, we would go outside and play, attend events with each other, go to each other's homes, even attended the same college. Sincere read exams for me. She also gave assistance with proofreading research papers making sure the formatting was correct. After graduating from college, we lost contact due to an adversity that occurred in Sincere's life. Thanks to social media we were back in touch again!

* (Childhood bestfriend Sincere, her daughter Tamia, and I)

Browsing Facebook on a beautiful day I ran across one of Winter's posts. I found out she was pregnant. Ironically the father of her child was the son of my childhood best friend. I smiled as I rushed to pick up the phone to contact Sincere. Once I heard her voice, I began explaining the story as to how Winter and I are acquainted sharing what I saw via Facebook. Sincere replied "Wow." Both responded "What a small world!" Winter had a baby girl of whom I'm proud and honor to be the god mother of such a bundle of joy. As Star's god mother, I will have a sincere interest in the child's upbringing and personal development, and should anything happen to her parents, I would take care of her as a godmother is supposed to do. I will be a good listener, encourage her to grow in faith, and love as she's taught to live as a Christian. I have and will always commit time praying for life's challenges that may arise in Star's life. If she needs food or shelter, I am here. Star will be shown how to make wise choices in life such as resisting temptation, how to deal with peer pressure when she gets older, along with being kind and compassionate towards others.

Throughout your life, god mommy shall continue to shower you with many blessings. I enjoy spending quality time with my god baby, the videos, hugs, phone calls, pictures, particularly holidays, birthdays, and family gatherings. I love watching her mature as she develops personality and self-identity of becoming her own person. I can remember when I tailored a gift bag for Easter that's age appropriate with clothes, socks, head bands, an Easter bunny, a bear, apple sauce, cheese curls, animal crackers, sippy cup, and a hooded bath towel that her god brother wanted his god sister to have.   She loved the gift bag especially, the red outfit as her grandmother who is my childhood best friend describes the look on her face that I wish I could have seen. It was amazing to see how she reacted when she saw the outfit being so young. Kids never cease to amaze me! My princess, Star will know that she can always count on god mommy at all times. God mommy wants you to know that I will always love and be here for you. You will always hold a special place in my heart!

* (Winter, holding her daughter Star)

* (Me holding Star)

Sincere new that Winter meant the world to me and I missed her so much. Bridging the gap, Sincere decided to have a Christmas party at her brand-new home in December 2016. I was so happy for her. Attendees at the party were Sincere, her daughter Tamia and son Peter, Winter, Star, a couple of friends, Joshua and myself. Winter and I made eye contact, hugged each other tightly as we conversed for hours. I felt so special. It was as if I was reunified with my other daughter I never had. I let her know as I always have that I love you and will always be here for you as long as you allow me too, teary eyed and all. As best friends, we were there through thick and thin, encouraged one another to stand strong no matter what obstacles we face in life. Sincere believes if she did not talk to me, she doesn't know where she would be. She said I was her motivation and inspiration to continue on. I let nothing stop me from doing what I want to do. I put my mind to it and just do it. Even though you are blind, that within itself is amazing!

6

SEVENTY YEAR OLD MAN
STILL KNOCKING BOOTS

A seasoned man had his best friend and best friend's girlfriend reside with him in his home. One evening the seventy-year-old man and his best friend girlfriend headed to Florida on a friendly excursion. Well, the 70-year-old man just happens to be my grandfather. Jerry and Terry had a wonderful time on their trip. They viewed the state, visited a jazz restaurant, ate dinner, came back to the hotel and started knocking boots.

Mind you this woman who is the best friend's girlfriend, is the one he is screwing. Now Terry and Jerry are an inter-racial couple. She's a woman in her thirty's. My grandfather liked them young, different sizes, shapes, and cultural backgrounds. As long as they had a vagina with a hole that his penis could go in that was alright with him. I guess that nut felt real good to both of them because it enters Terry's vagina and a child was conceived. Best friend's girlfriend supposed to have been on an excursion with his friend. How do you explain that one? It's the Jerry Springer show…. the two get married and became one. When the two returned home they informed everyone of marriage and pregnancy. I know the best friend Al felt some type of way. Al was upset and eventually moved out.

A year later and more knocking boots, getting his thrills on, and oops there it is… Another child was born. As grandpop told me "I didn't know it still worked." "It just went boop boop, there it goes." I said "WHAT?" and my mother, sister Sarah, and I started laughing. This time, Terry said this one was my grandfather's child. We all know that both are his children. Terry lead Al to believe the baby was his. However, all along, she was my grandfather's child. The girls are beautiful. Terry knew what she was doing. She used those old men to get pregnant so they could take care of her and her children.

Once the kids got older, they were home schooled and sheltered for some time. Then Terry decided that she and the kids were moving to TN with another man that she was interested in. Jerry was hurt. Karma will hit you in the face every time. What goes around comes around. Its 10 times worse when you're on the receiving end.

One day Jerry received a phone call from TN saying that Terry is in the hospital. He had to make arrangements to take off of work to go down and pick the girls up. My grandfather was an upholsterer and did upholstery in a shop re-upholstering furniture for residential homes and businesses. I believe he stayed there for a couple of weeks. Terry passed away and he brought the kids back home.

After the family came back home, the girls asked if they could be enrolled in school. Jerry agreed to enroll them. This was a difficult time for the girls because they were sheltered for so long. After a while they adjusted well.

My mother was an only child for a long time until her sister Nin from Vietnam was birthed. She and my mom are 10 years apart. Grandpop met Nin's Mother being in the military. He served in the Vietnam War along with the army. My mother's mother was an African American woman mixed with Indian. Papa was a rolling stone. Wherever he played was his home. He loved my grandmother's cooking and looked forward to coming to dinner on Sunday. My grandfather was diagnosed with a terminal illness and while in the nursing home, he flirted with the nurses.

Grandpop was in denial for a long time but one day he accepted the realization that he was sick. While in denial, he thought he could drive even when the doctors told him he couldn't. When your loved ones are up in age and set in their ways, it's hard to get them to listen. His ability to think affected daily functioning, motivation decreased, and emotional problems occurred. He only wanted to stay at his house. He gave the family a fit about living in the nursing facility. Grandpop raised so much cane that the nurses called my mother to asked if the family could come to speak with him and calm him down. My sister Sarah and I went to visit him. As we were explaining that he had to stay there due to his condition, he cursed us out. He told us to, "get the hell out of here!" As he's saying this he's coming towards Sarah in his wheel chair as if he was going to hit her stating "I'll bop you." Once he calmed down we put him in a cab and sent him home. He was there around a couple of weeks before he was placed back in the nursing facility. My mother did all she could to provide for her father. At times, it was very stressful, managing a sickly father and raising two teenage girls. Grandpop apologized to both of us. Grandpop wanted me to know that he wasn't mad with me. He understood that I was trying to help him. He survived for years before crossing to the other side. His children graduated with their high school diplomas and are doing well.

7

LOVE, GOD AIN'T DONE WITH ME YET

Love is a strong affection for someone. Love is an intense feeling of deep affection, a great interest in pleasure of something, a person or thing that one loves. Love is a risk that one can take and the risk may turn out to be great. But what if the risk is not so great? Our emotions are affected and we have to find a way to cope as we get over those hurtful feelings.

Let me tell ya how a man is ta show ya love

Read below so that you know

Love is an emotion

Especially from a man of my dreams that makes you cum

Like an explosion

The man who I've been searching for, the apple of my eye

The love of my life, one who makes you quiver as my body shakes

Oh, baby multiple orgasms, yes, I can take

As our body yearns through the twists and turns

Caressing me gently only you can discern

In the vagina, hitting the walls

Here penis, you can have it all!

A sensation like no other occurs like never before

One that will make you come back for more

An emotion of pleasure

One I will always treasure

Hear my command

Until you have this experience child, you just won't understand!!!!

You gotta excuse me

You see

I'm just trying to keep it real!

And show you sex is the deal!

The blind has to get her needs fulfill too

Remember, I'm human just like you!

God ain't done with me yet uniquely bless

I'm still a work in progress

Love displays action,

Just like satisfaction

From a true man whose your confidant

Sharing your deepest secrets with your best friend

One who will be with you to endure until the end

Hurts, disappointments, I'll forgive

Only our hearts will mend

The key to a relationship is sex, finance, and communication

So, find a man to flex you with romance yet filled with creation

Presenting my trials and tribulations has afforded the opportunity to share my testimony to bless someone else. You may have faced the same challenges that I had to overcome like depression, setbacks, losing loved ones, harassment, discrimination, failure to promote, failure to provide reasonable accommodations in the workplace filled with hostility. Going through the state of great suffering in the body and mind due to intimate or romantic relationships that lead to devastation, heartache, feeling numb.

Despite the tests, God had me become the champion. Once I realized I could not handle these battles on my own. I decided to turn them over to the Lord because the battle is not mine, it's the Lord's, referenced in 2 Chronicles 20: 15. Then God provided the resources. Being able to seek mental health treatment allowed me to bounce back to my vibrant self. I began to pray, humble myself, while seeking God's face in the midst of all that I was going through because I knew prayer work.

Being blind raising children doesn't mean you aren't capable of caring for children. The blind should be treated just like the sighted not having to worry about facing barriers such as having their child removed from the home due to society's biases or lack of education. Blind parents are nurturers, loving, trustworthy and we ensure that our children's needs are met. I was blessed. I never had to experience my child being removed from the home. However, I am the one who is used to encourage others who had to face such excruciation along with the National Federation of the Blind. I was the blind one, a legal guardian of my relatives. According to 2 Chronicles 7: 14 "If my people who are called by my name will humble themselves and pray, seek my face, and turn from their wicked ways. I will hear from heaven. I'll forgive their sin and heal their land." We must remain humble and pray continuously no matter what comes our way. Even with the loss of a loved one, trust that God will see you through. Depression is real. Hurt pain, you just can't deal. Help is on the way and you will say," I know a God who is able to heal!"

Sharing my testimonial gave me the chance to enlighten all who come in contact with this amazing memoir. I hope each and every one of you received an eye opener, at times, you may have wept, or laughed. I pray that you were inspired, motivated, and encouraged. You don't know my story like I know my story. You don't know the pain I've been through. Remember, my testimony is used to be a blessing to someone else.

Uniquely blessed in my own way! I am set apart by God. His hands are on me for a specific purpose. Romans 8: 28, "And we know that all things work together for good to them that love God to them who are called according to his purpose."

* (Family Collage)

* (Great Grandma Millie, Aunt Jamaica, Grandma Ruth, Uncle John)

ABOUT THE AUTHOR

Sherria Young a.k.a Uniquely Blessed1 may have lost her sight, but she has not lost her love of life. She has achieved many feats, including several college degrees, raising a son as a single mother, a choral songstress, and now author. God Ain't Done with me Yet was written as a testimony so that others may be inspired, motivated, encouraged as well as educated.

Made in the USA
San Bernardino, CA
12 October 2018